AF593452

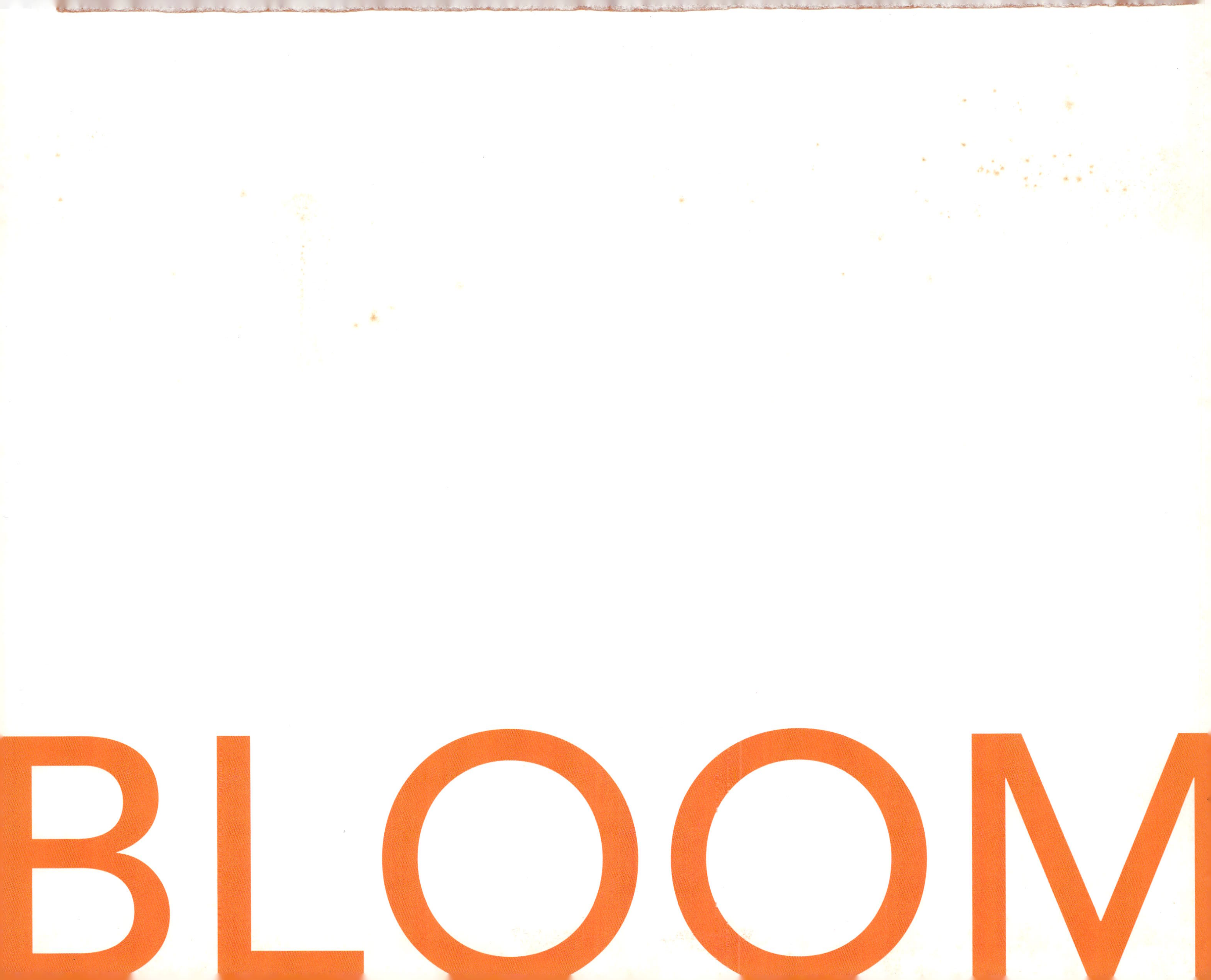
BLOOM

BLO

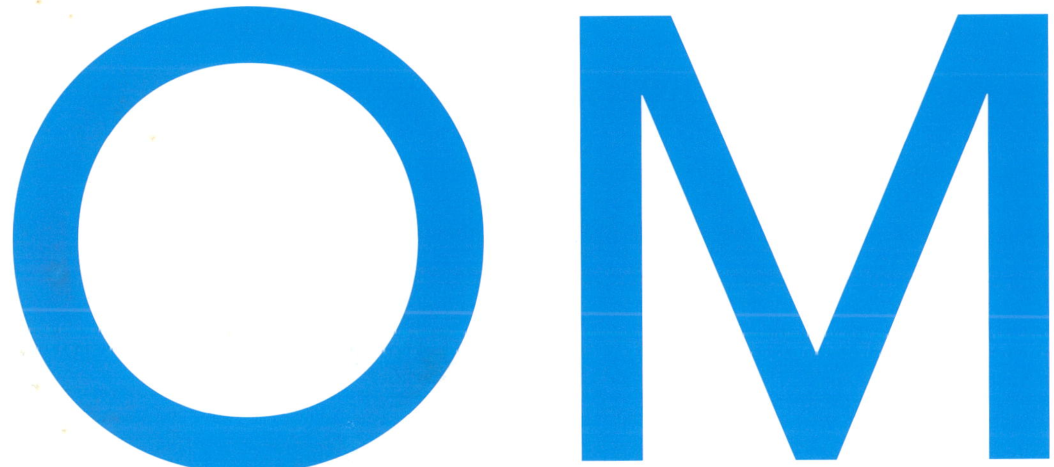

PAUL SOLBERG

EDITED
CHRISTOPHER MAKOS

PREFACE
RALPH PUCCI

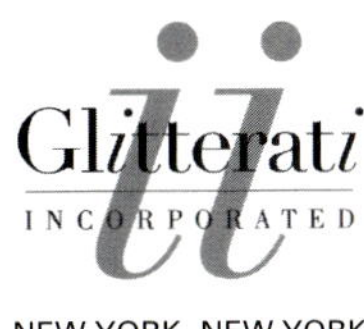

NEW YORK, NEW YORK

DEDICATED TO: My parents, Mary and Conrad Solberg, who have stayed on-board through sun and storm; for their unwavering support and love.

SPECIAL THANKS: Christopher Makos, Marta Hallett, Pablo Garcia Perez, Mark Montgomery, Stephen Kinsella, Ralph Pucci, Olivier Giugni, Dotson Rader, Inmaculada Lladro, Francisco Reyes Medina, Luis Christophe, Harald Johnson, Charlie Rose, Emilio Saliquet, Borjas Bas, Dorothy Blau, Glenn Albin, Agatha Ruiz de la Prada, Patrick McMullan, Isabelle and Philip del Grange, Edmond Franco, Pilar Vico, The Tourist Board of Spain, John D'Aleo, Jonay Cogollos van der Linden, Andy Merhi, Jonas Neilson, Paul Lambert, Vera Wang, Tom Conley, James Maharg, Brian Sawyer, James Moore, John Batchelor, Mark Sink, Chris Madkour, Nancy Price, Mick Kopetsky, Dale Rozmiarek, Genevieve Maquinay, Christian Deseglise, Dalia Simmons, Hewlett Packard, Tim Allis, *In Style Magazine*, Central Park Conservatory, Krissy Gutroff, W Hotels, Jeffrey Serafini, Fischer and Page, *Elle Décor*, Paolo Antonelli, Rosemary Feitelberg, Robert DuGrenier, Isabelle Huppert, Rob Dukes, Troy Taylor, Christian Roth, Eric Domege, Christian Deseglise, Anna Felt, Sam Shahid, Barbara and Emmett Dowdal, Megan Dowdal-Osborn, Ryan Solberg, Sally Mueller, Marlee and Ed Nelson, Byron and Georgie Doyle, George Krol, Jean Kinsella, Patricia, Billy and John O'Brien, Gregg Ventra, Frank Andolino, Peter Wise, Sue Olmos, Luisa Cerutti, Nicki Lindheimer, Dean Mellon, Dave Ouyang, Charlotte, Catherine Enright, Louise Baudoin, Michael Foster, Michael Rawson, Vernyl Pederson, Anne Cohen, Paul Washington, James Huniford, Carmen Calvo, Kathleen Tripp, Martin Cis, Neil Rasmus, Lisa Silhanek, Man Ray, Max Ernst, Richard Avedon, Alfred Stieglitz, Shaun Gunderson, my family, and the staff at L'Olivier Floral Atelier.

Their music inspires... Blossom Dearie, Cole Porter, Blondie, Dee Dee Bridgewater, Bjork, Sara Vaughan, Etta James, Carmen McRae, Diana Krall, Henry Mancini, George Michael, Nina Simone, Elis Regina, Debbie Harry, Cal Tjader, Mina, Nancy Wilson, Sheryl Crow, Yma Sumac, Julie London, Ephraim Lewis, Anita O'Day, Jill Scott, Miles Davis, Gal Costa, K.D. Lang, Gilberto Gil, Stan Getz, Bebel Gilberto and her parents, Jobim, Angie Stone, Stan Getz, Mike Flowers.

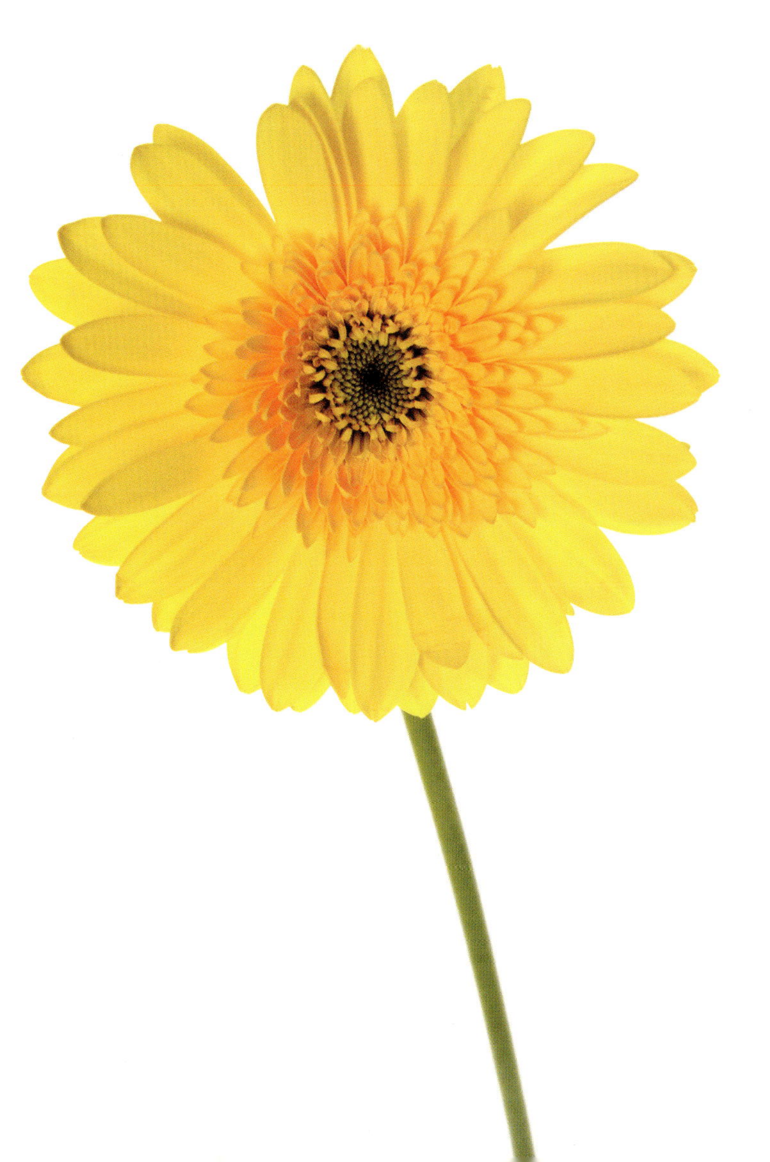

CONTENTS

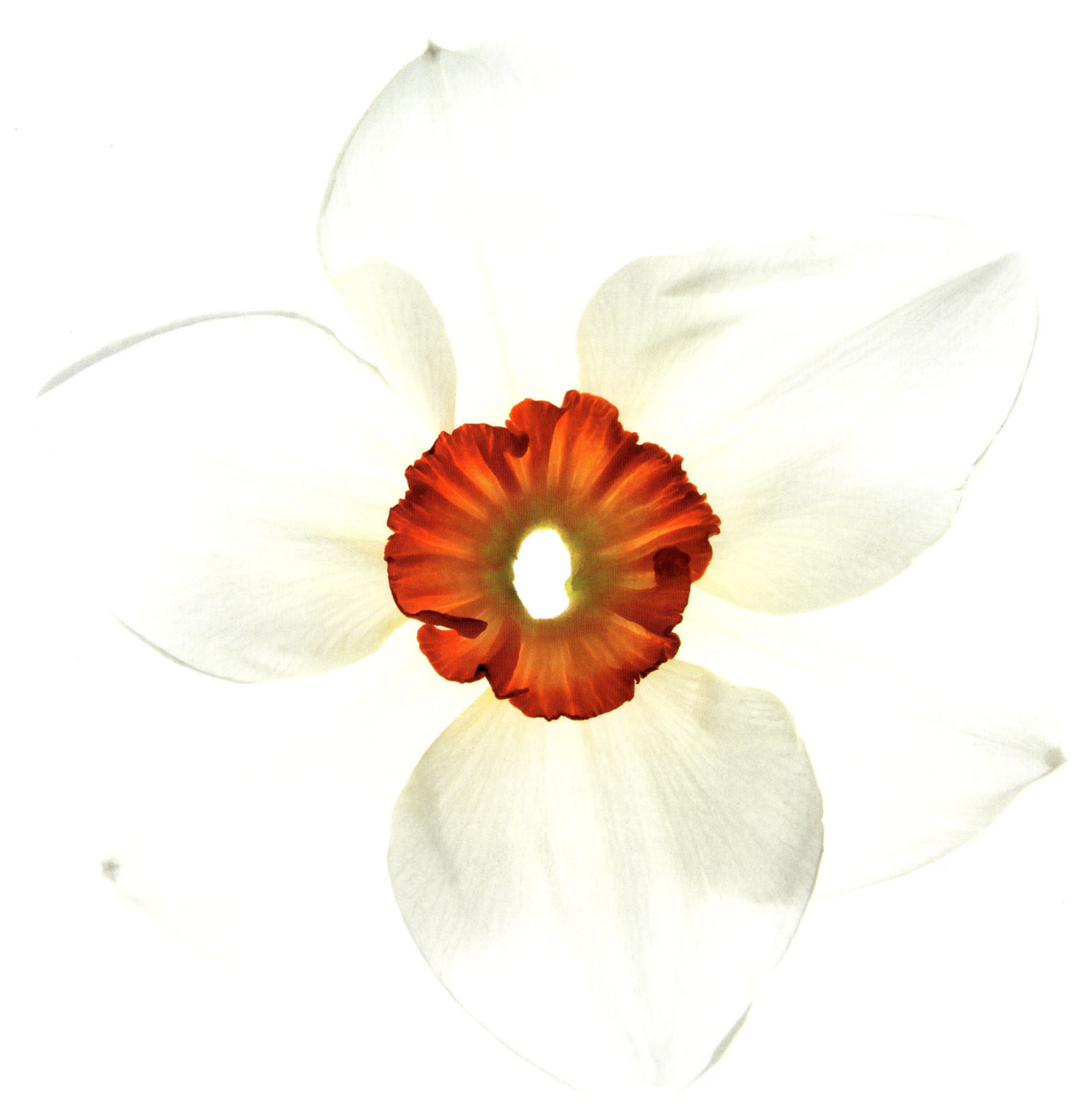

PrefaceRalphPucci

When Christopher Makos asked me to take a look at the photography of his friend, Paul Solberg, I could hear the excitement in his voice. It must be something unique and special for Chris to make a call, especially for the work of another photographer! I was not familiar with Paul's photography, but I am always looking for break-through and talented artists, designers, photographers–-someone who has something "new to say." The subject matter, flowers, also interested me–for the obvious reason, beauty–but also because my last gallery exhibition of a show on the subject of flowers, in 2000, had been amazingly successful.

Could Paul have come up with a new slant on this over-exposed topic? The answer is, yes.

After seeing Paul's work, Chris immediately called to ask me what I thought. He said there was going to be a book on the work coming out fall of 2005 and would I like to write the preface. I was honored, and said yes.

I wanted the preface to the book to have a similar feel to that I strive for with my mannequin, furniture, and art presentations: unpretentious, understated, almost spare. I started thinking of words, names, places, that reminded me of Paul's photography.

First, I wrote down *fresh, modern, clean*, and then for some reason, *Stan Getz,* the incredible saxophone player from the 1950's / 60's came into my head. The rest followed: *Samba, Original, Berries, Summer, Bill Evans, Irving Penn, Miami, New, Cool, Miles Davis, Jazz, Water, Corral, Astrid Gilberto, Italy, Sorbet, Barbados, Henri Matisse, Sexy, Translucent, Richard Meier, Wow, Arne Jacobsen, Yoga, Figs, India, Strawberry Fields, De Witte Lelie, Richard Gluckman, Brazil, Jelly Beans, Luis Barragan, John Pawson, Ballet, Jade, Ellsworth Kelly, Bel Air Hotel, New, Pure, Jens Risom, Virginal, White, Color, Cy Twombly, Spring, Tomatoes, Gaetano Velesco, Light, Flute, Herbie Mann, Lemons, Waves, Passion, Napa Valley, Museum of Modern Art*. I could go on and on, but then I thought it would be interesting if after viewing this amazing work of Paul's for you, the reader, to continue this funny little word / name game. Have fun!

Ralph Pucci, New York

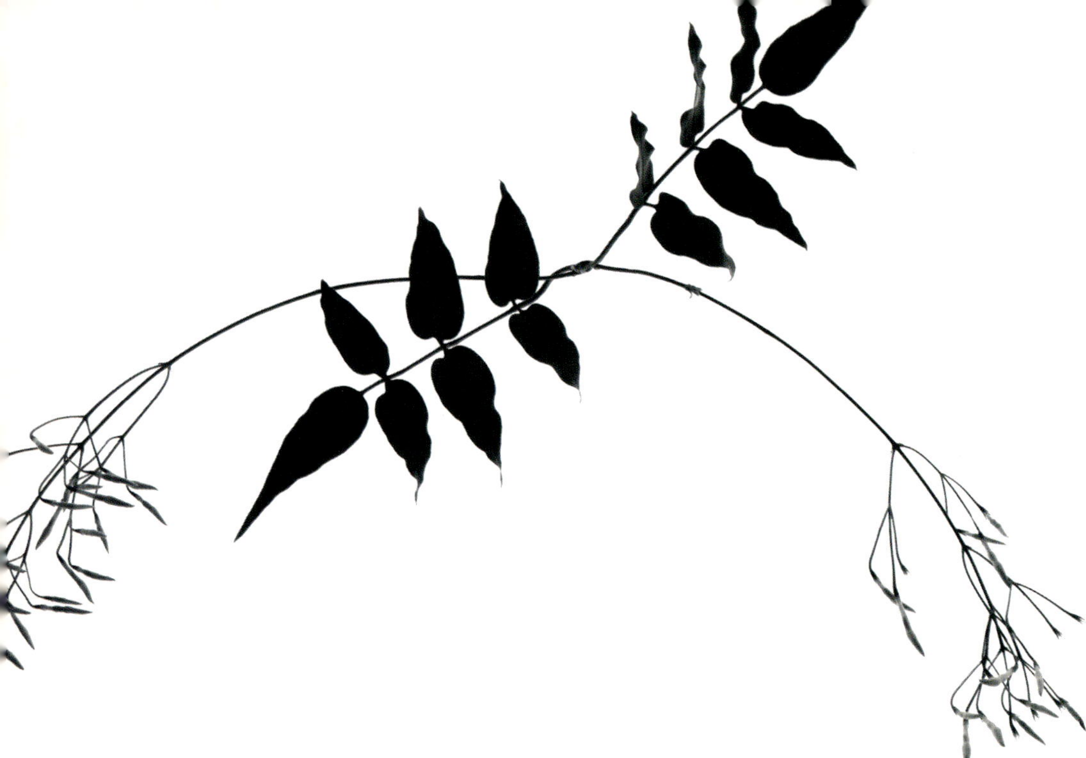

ForewordChristopherMakos

I met Paul Solberg during the summer of 2004. I had just come back to New York from Lanzorate, one of the Canary Islands, when I was introduced to him by a mutual friend. Within moments I was enthusiastically telling him about the beauty of the island of Lanzorate and the photographs I had taken there. As I rattled on, Paul took a small notebook out of his pocket and made a note to himself about the place I was describing. This small, unself–conscious gesture was the initial glimpse I had of his intense curiosity about life. That quality–the hunger to know coupled with a love of beauty and a sense of wonder, the other gifts that he possesses–define an artist's sensibility.

Paul is always questioning himself, but he seems to know that the answers are only found through real experience. At the beginning of our friendship Paul was working on Wall Street for an investment firm. He worked hard, long hours, and he was very good at what he did. But the Paul Solberg I quickly got to know was not at all a person who shared the values of "moneyland." He was an alien there, ill-at-ease. He knew who he was inside, he knew himself, but was still searching for the way to become the person he was meant to be. And he knew this: That person did not belong in an office on Wall Street.

Soon Paul and I started taking bicycle day-trips around New York, and then we went on longer car trips outside the city. It was during those times that I learned of Paul's immense love of photography; how it has been with him since he was a teenager growing up in Minnesota. He was a photographer, and that is what he was always meant to be. It was as simple and as difficult a fact as that, and he knew it.

That summer I had just converted to digital photography after 25 years of shooting on film. Paul kept asking me questions about digital photography. I explained how a

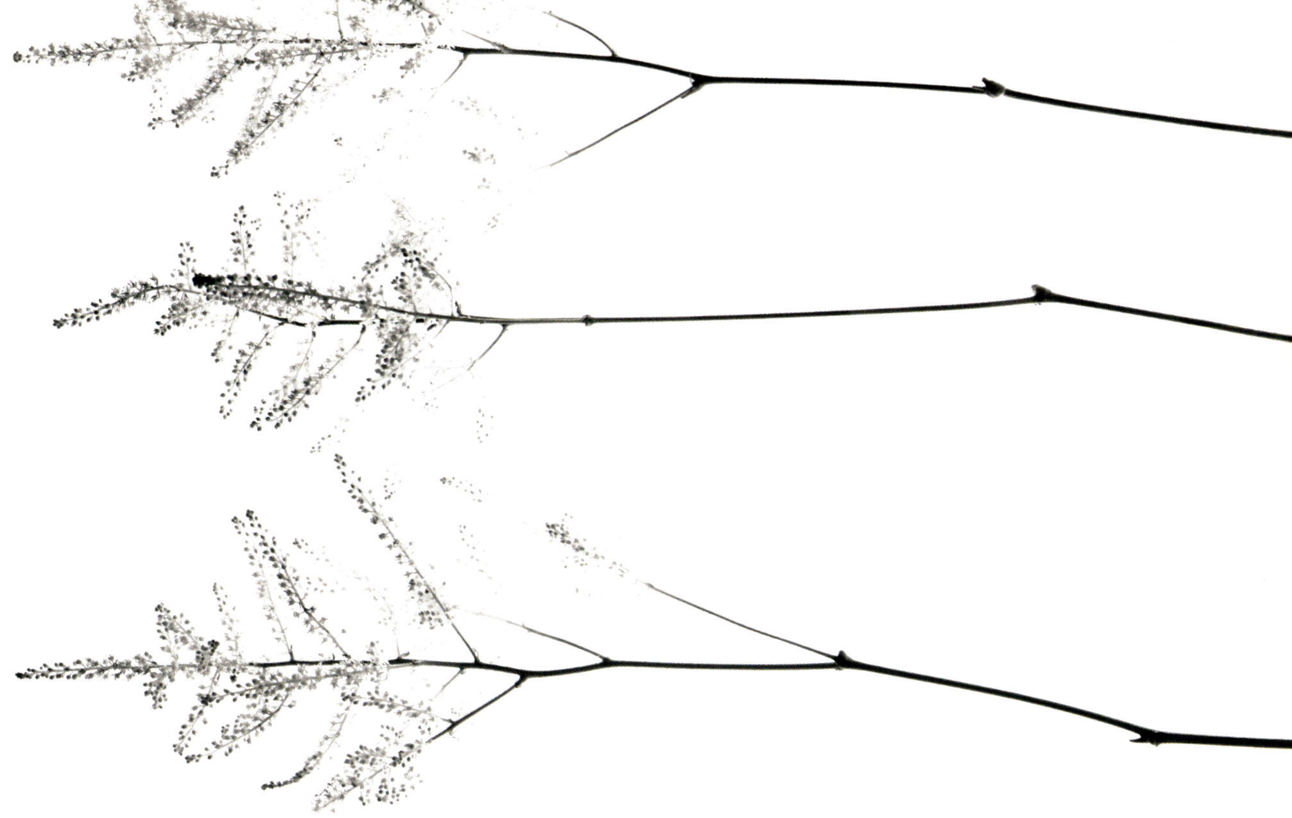

photographer's efficiency was increased several fold with digital technology because of the instantaneous connection between being able to see and select images.

It gave you a better eye and more command. There was no real lag any more from the moment you captured a picture to the moment you edited it. Time was radically compressed, and because of it photography was set free. Digital cameras made photography a more creative, less wasteful, more malleable art. You could really focus on how to see and edit images through your lens. It gave a new immediacy, without the three-day delay (or more) you experienced with traditional analog film.

Paul watched as I grew to love my new seeing machine. He decided to get one himself. In less than a year, using a digital camera and his extraordinary ability to see and capture natural beauty, he produced this amazing collection of elegant, painterly, and unforgettable pictures.

Flowers are among the most photographed of subjects, and that's why they may be the toughest objects to see in a new way. They are too familiar, even banal. But, here in these exquisite pictures in **BLOOM**, Paul Solberg makes flowers astonish us with wonder again.

We see their images gloriously captured in these pages as we have never seen flowers before–and their portraits are breathtakingly beautiful.

Paul always speaks about what bad vision he has. With his eye doctors giving him grim reports about his eyes, I say to the eye doctors: Just take a look at Paul's photographs. He has *perfect* vision.

Christopher Makos, New York City

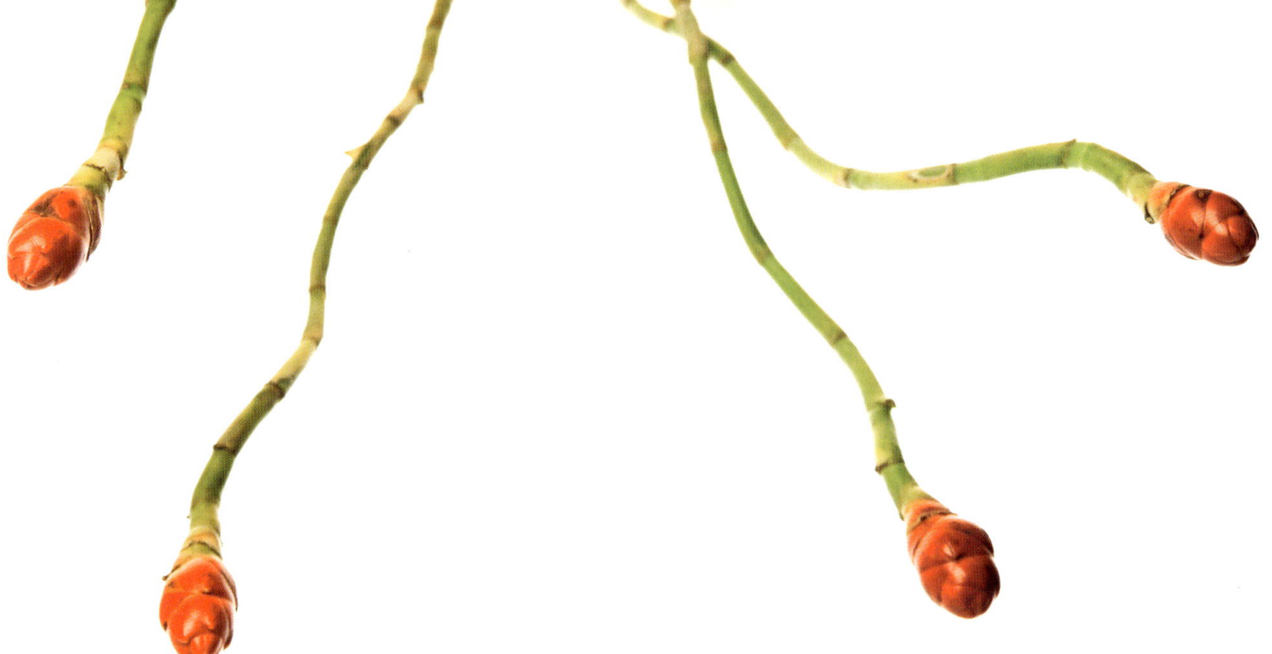

Art and Soul

"Paul, stop staring!" I heard that a lot as a kid. I have a vivid memory of being no more than eight years old on the front porch of our neighbor's house, where I spent many summer days. The mother of the house was a rich character with lots of intrigue. She would sit on the porch for the entire summer, and I would watch her, much to her alarm. The way her kind, sad eyes tried to follow her children playing in the front yard as she burned through packs of cigarettes and cheap champagne, wondering where her life had gone. I'd carefully watch her laugh, separating the real from the unreal. "Paul, stop staring!"

Later on, the camera gave me the license to watch people without frightening them. Looking back, it began, I suppose, in show choir, when I was a proud member of a pack of God-fearing Minnesota teens who set off to entertain Japan over the holiday season, whether Japan liked it or not. My Dad, responding to my high enthusiasm, strapped me down with pounds of old professional camera equipment around my neck, when cameras were made of metal. I proudly dragged the long lenses and camera accessories through the subways of Tokyo, much to the wicked amusement of my fellow chorus members. I laughed *with* them, as I was blissfully distracted by this new private playland, found in the viewfinder of the camera.

College-age, I stayed on the creative sidelines. To indulge in such effortless pleasure couldn't be right. In the world I grew up in, the business of "photography" or "creativity" was no real business, but rather a legitimate hobby. I was a mid-western Norwegian-American boy that followed the law of the land; if it's too easy, it's not right. So I became a "closeted" photographer, always taking pictures, but never allowing myself to be free.

Years later, after trying on a few ill-fitting hats as "a professional," I woke up on Wall Street. I was told I had been at my desk for years, working for the best in the business. The perfect firm. The perfect boss. I was dazed and confused. Where am I? Who am I? Although I apparently had a pulse, I didn't feel it. I had worn-out my welcome, wherever I was. After flirting with the front end of a cab one day after work, I realized I had no choice but to give my dream a chance. I left Wall Street, and Wall Street left me. Like any suppressed desire, the longer it's ignored, the stronger it grows. I was jobless, moneyless, and free! Within the same time, I serendipitously met Christopher Makos, who would be my champion in my quest to redefine the term "professional."

In April of last year, I was biking with a long-time friend,

Paul Solberg

artist Stephen Kinsella, when he introduced me to Christopher. After meeting Chris, time and experience took on a different shape. Personally and artistically, everything was new, revised, remixed. In the past, the word *serendipity* usually turned me off. I suppose when a part of your life is out of alignment, it's an optimist's term that can be offensive. The past nine months have been truly serendipitous for me, or just damn lucky. At 35-years-old, I've finally found the hat that fits; and, ironically, that candy-coated word seems to naturally emerge in describing my most authentic experience.

And so it went: Christopher Makos saw a picture I took of a barn. He immediately called art dealer Ralph Pucci to tell him that he must see my work. What work? The appointment was in one week and I had no material that was suitable to show to "The King of Art and Design." There was no time to schedule model visits or to consider elaborate concepts. Sure, I'd taken pictures of flowers outside my apartment window from time to time, but it was never a subject that got under my skin.

Suddenly under the pressure of this insane deadline, it seemed the natural choice. I ran to the nearest Korean deli, grabbed a bunch of flowers and locked myself in Makos' studio. Staying up through the night, the day, and night again, I lost myself in an euphoric creative haze.

The week was finished in a blink, and with my new portfolio in hand, I was off to the anticipated "interview" with Mr. Pucci. I laid out my work, and his response was, "Let's do a show!" Then, two days later, Chris showed the flowers to his publisher. She said, "Let's do a book!"

BLOOM is that book. It was my surprise pregnancy, with the perfect delivery. It's been the opposite of restraint. Pure indulgence. Perfect pleasure. No pain. Rapid growth. Instinctual. Intimate. Completely natural. And, of course, serendipitous. I'm proud of my first published offspring, one that I share with Christopher Makos. It couldn't have been conceived without him. From day one until the very end, he's treated **BLOOM** like his own.

This book is for those who have spent a lifetime surfing their dreams, for stubborn people like me who won't let their dreams die, and for those on the front porch, watching their dreams pass. I hope my visual story provides inspiration for freedom.

Paul Solberg, New York City

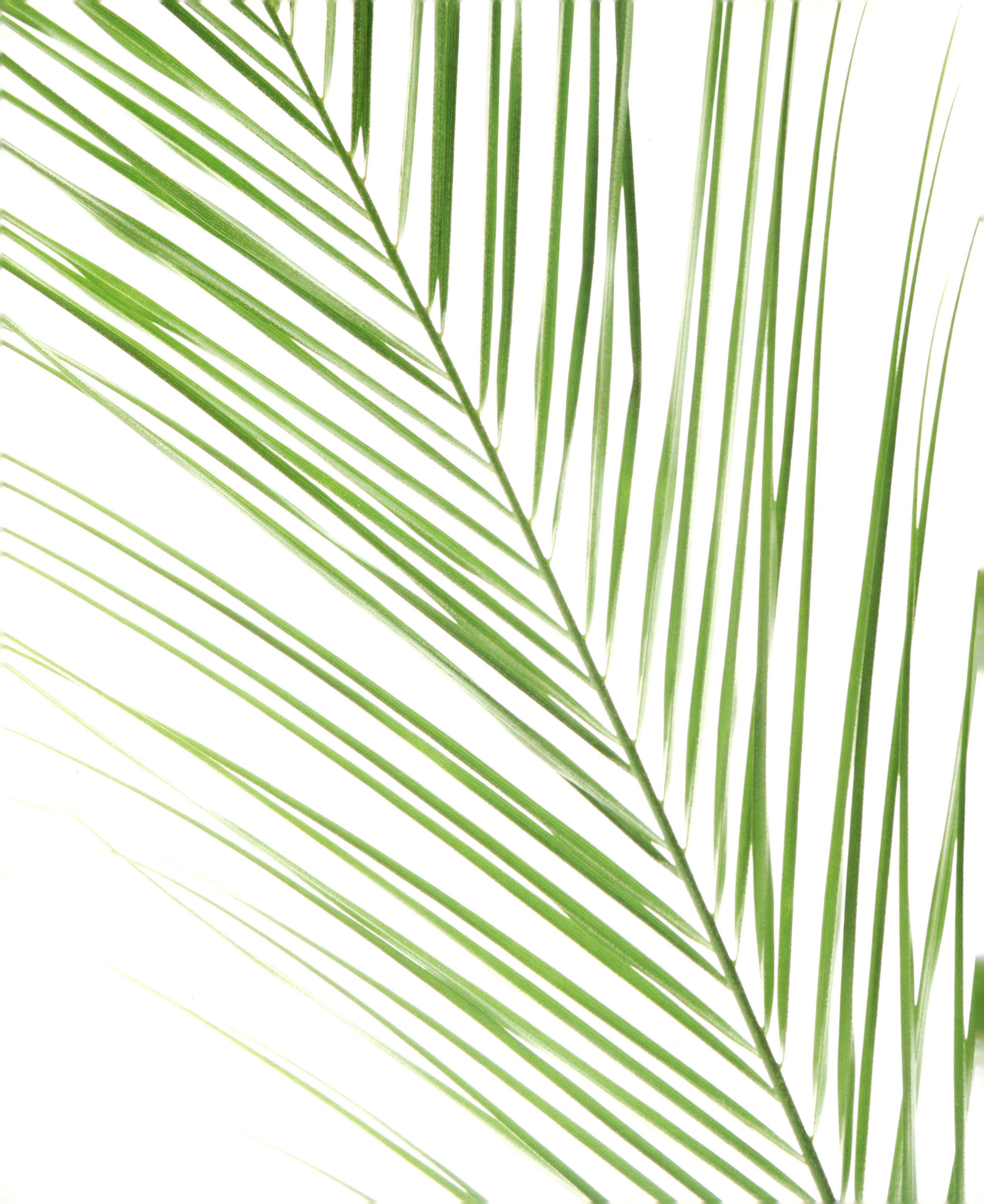

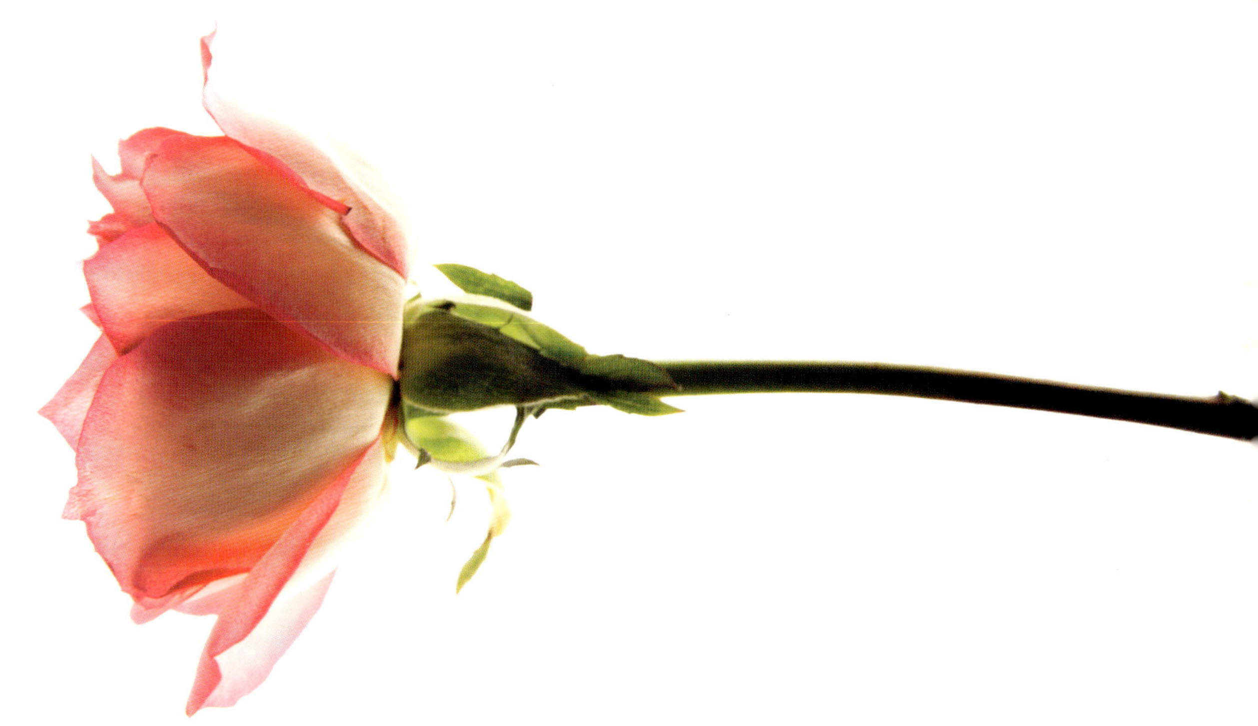

IMAGES

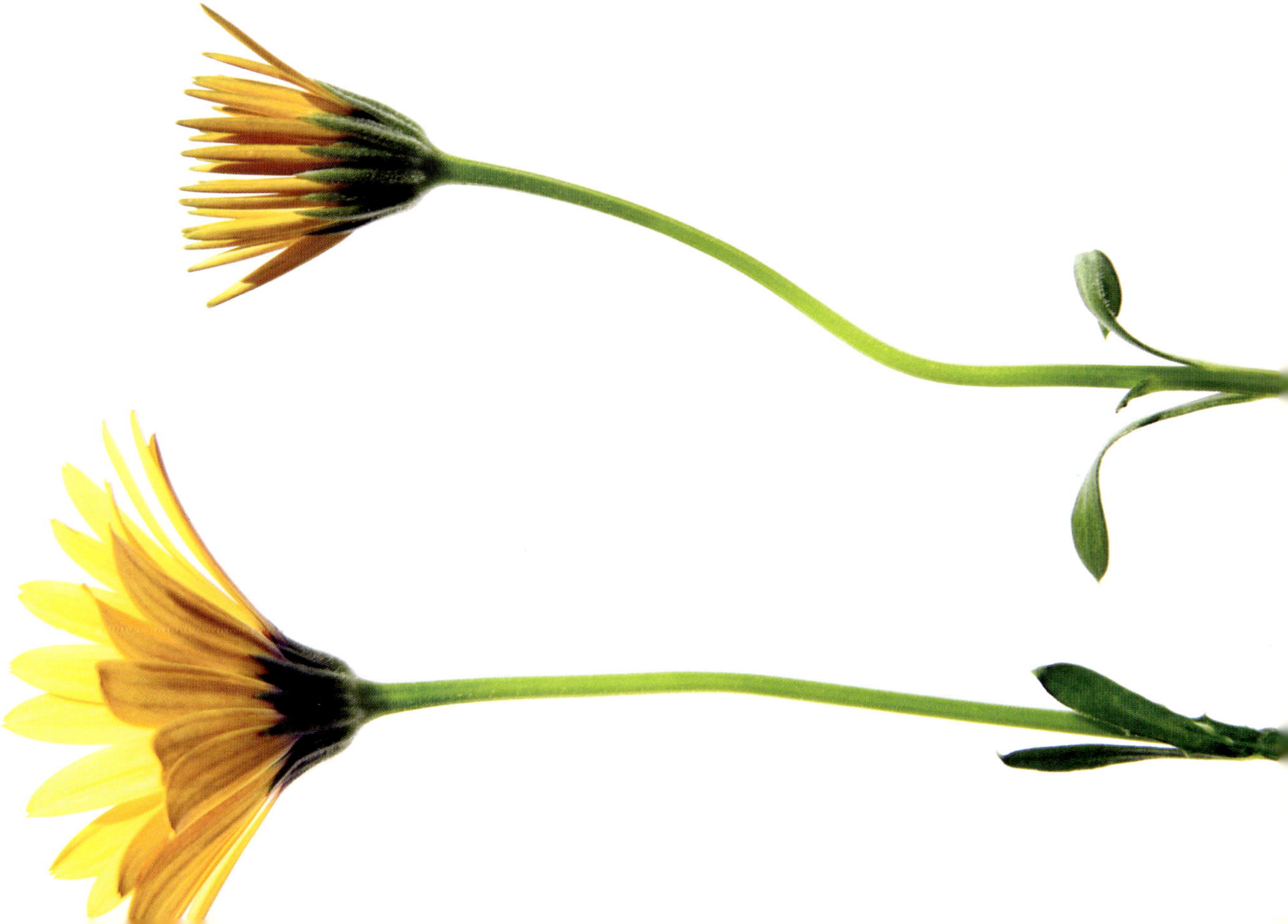

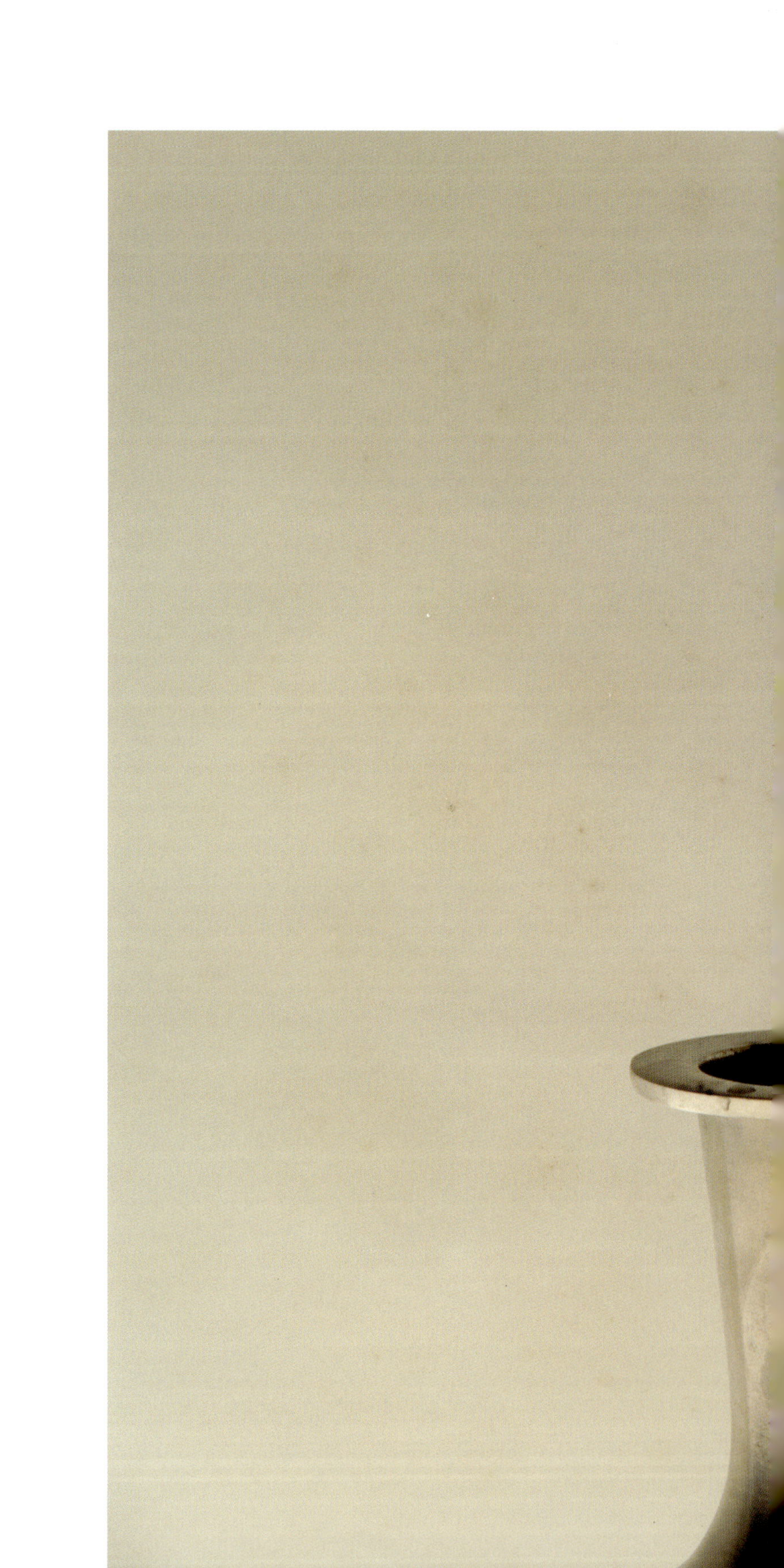

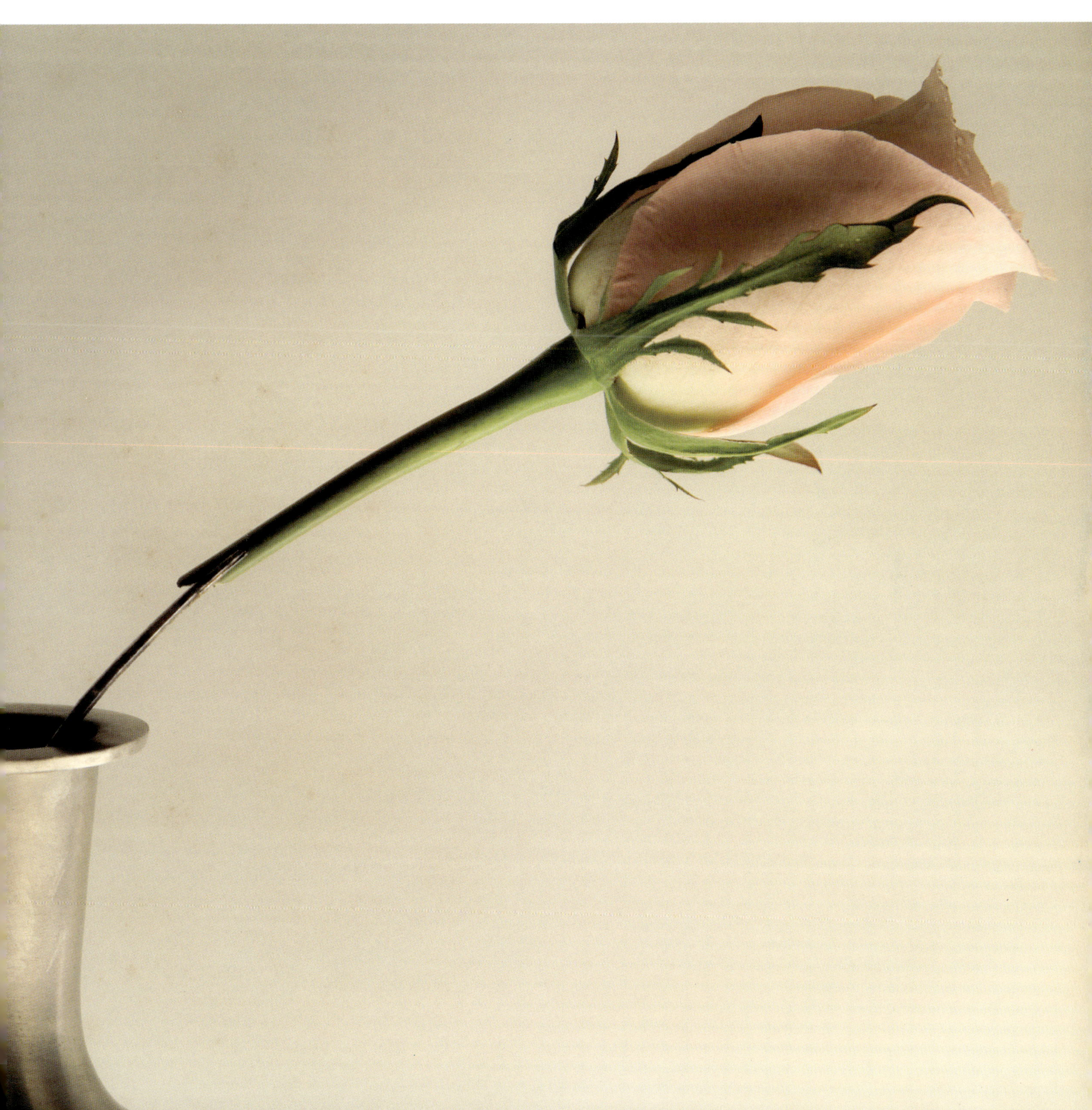

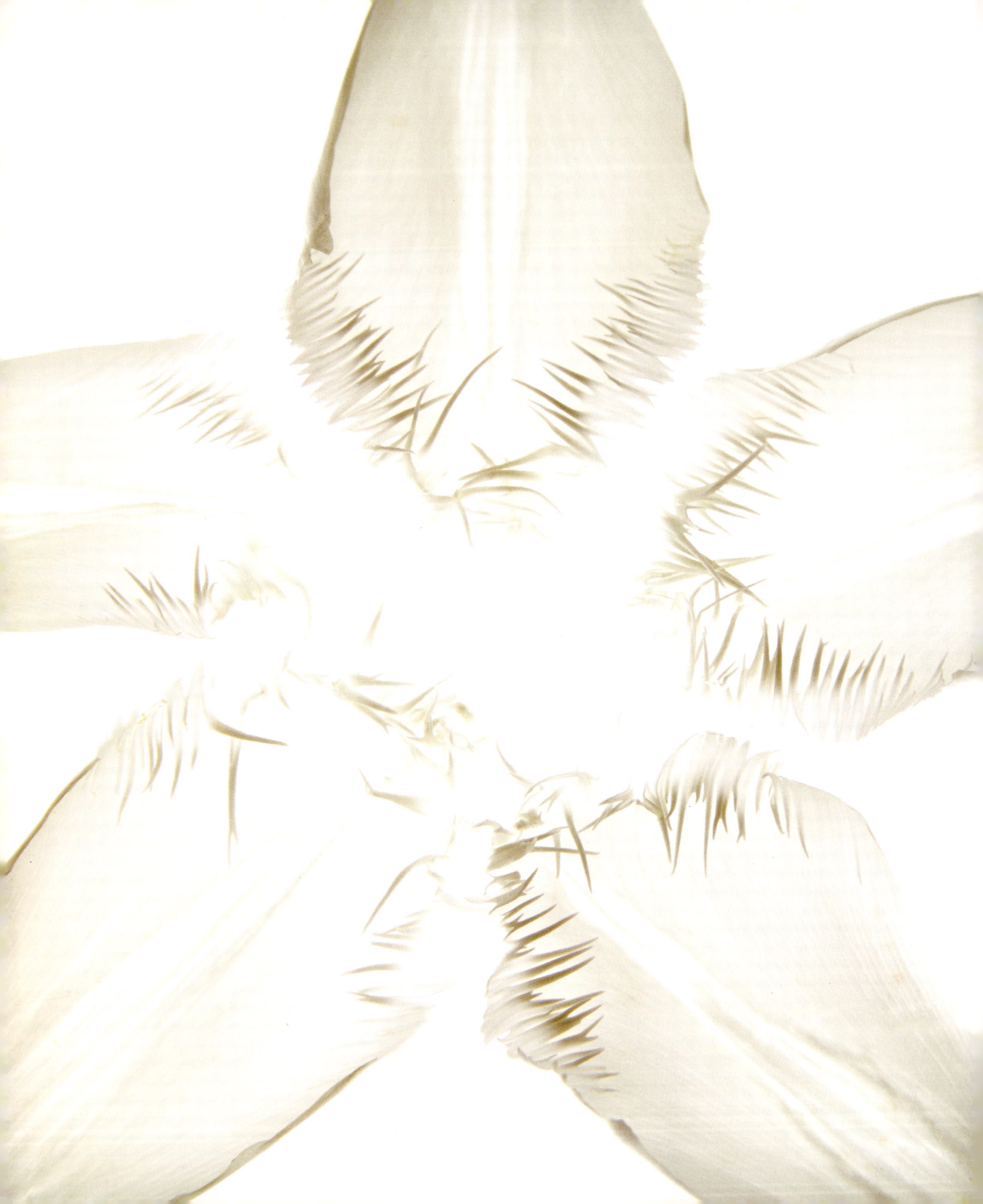

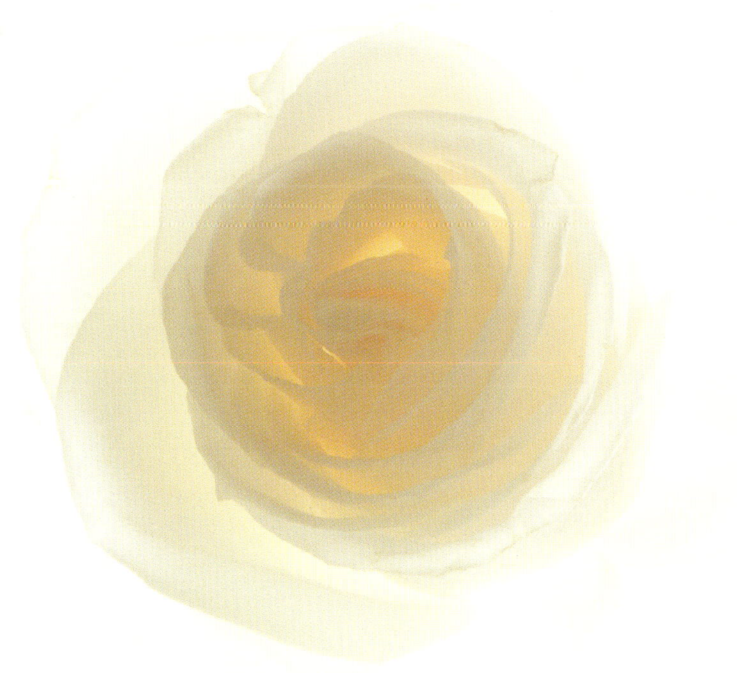

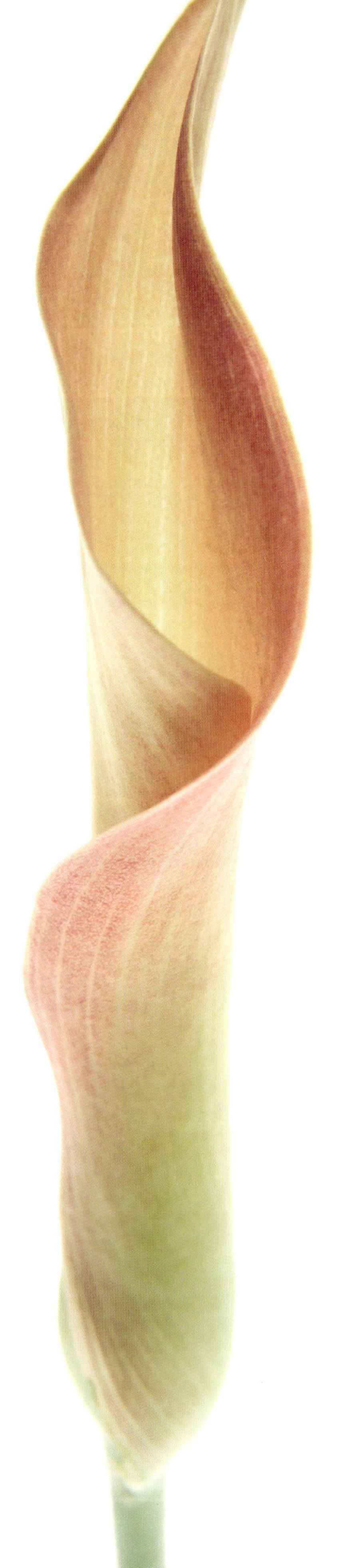

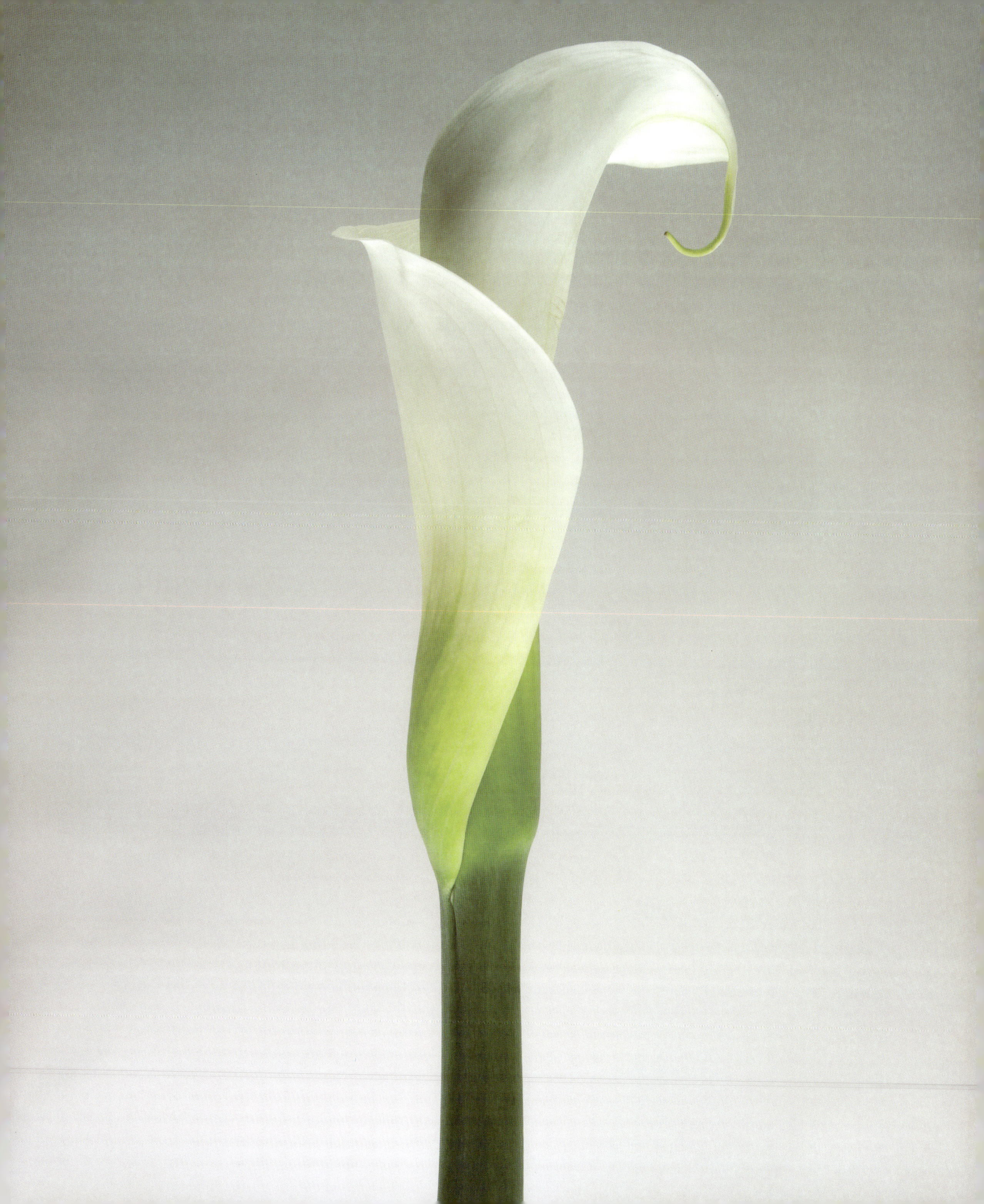

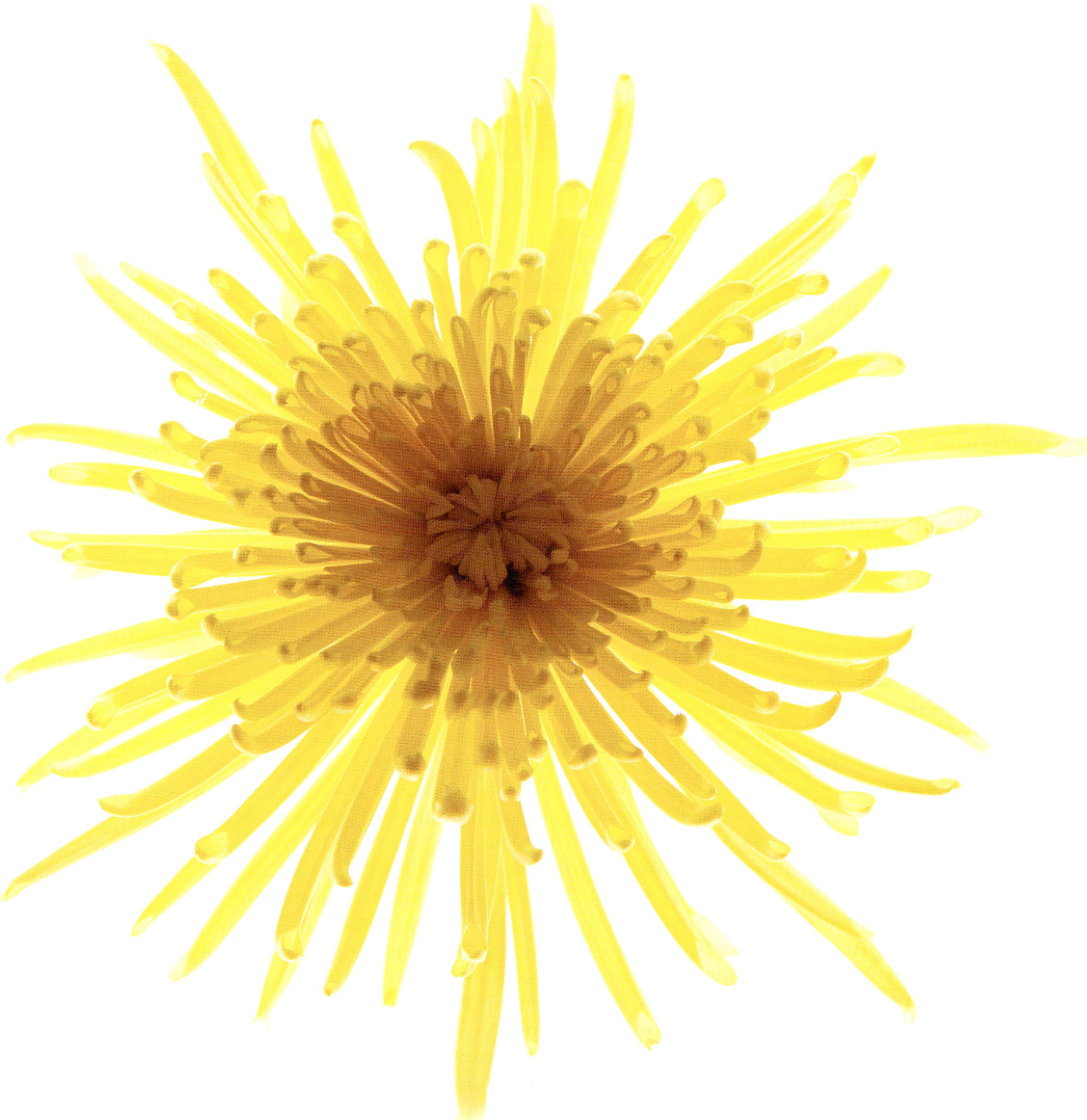

P20

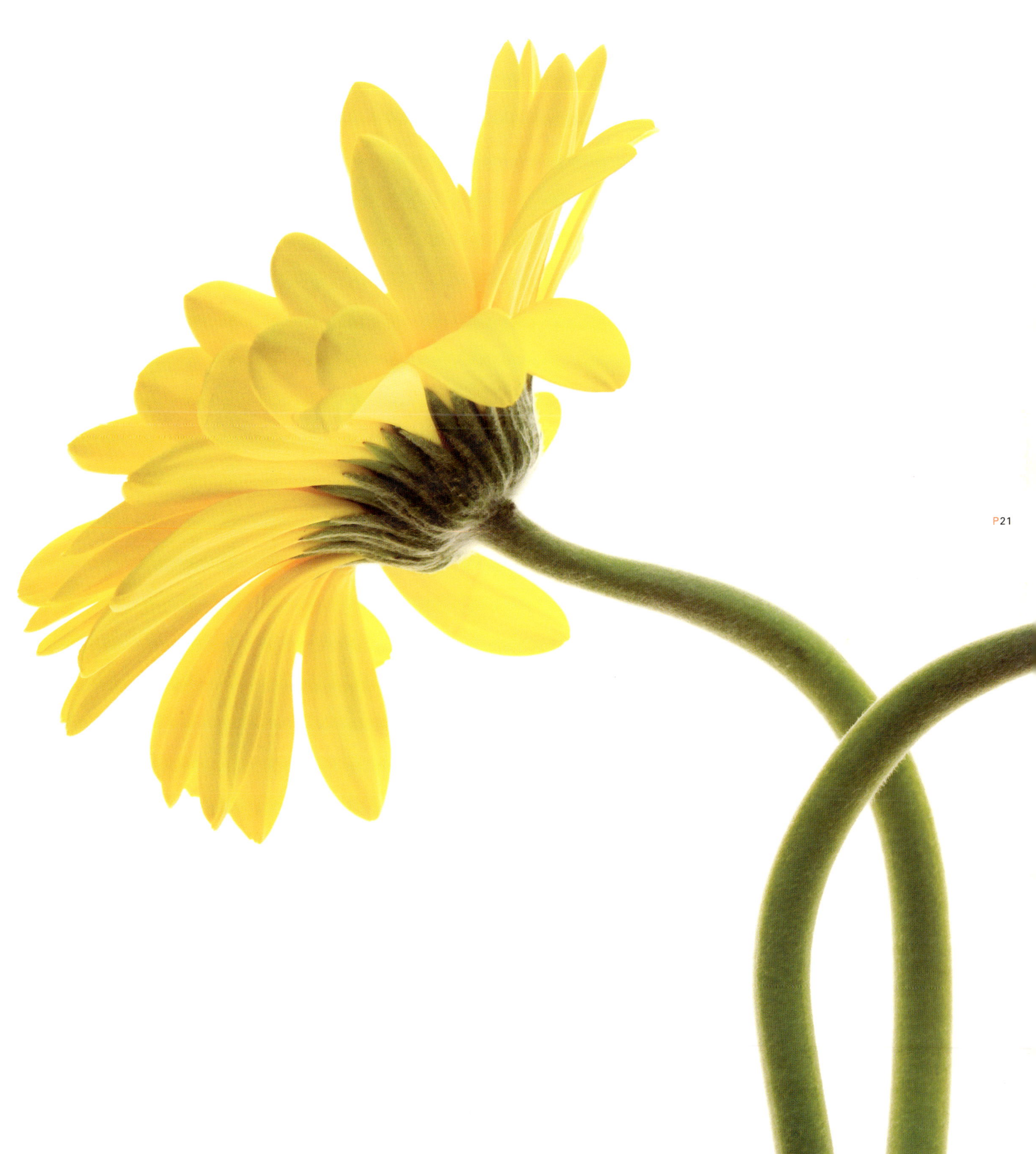

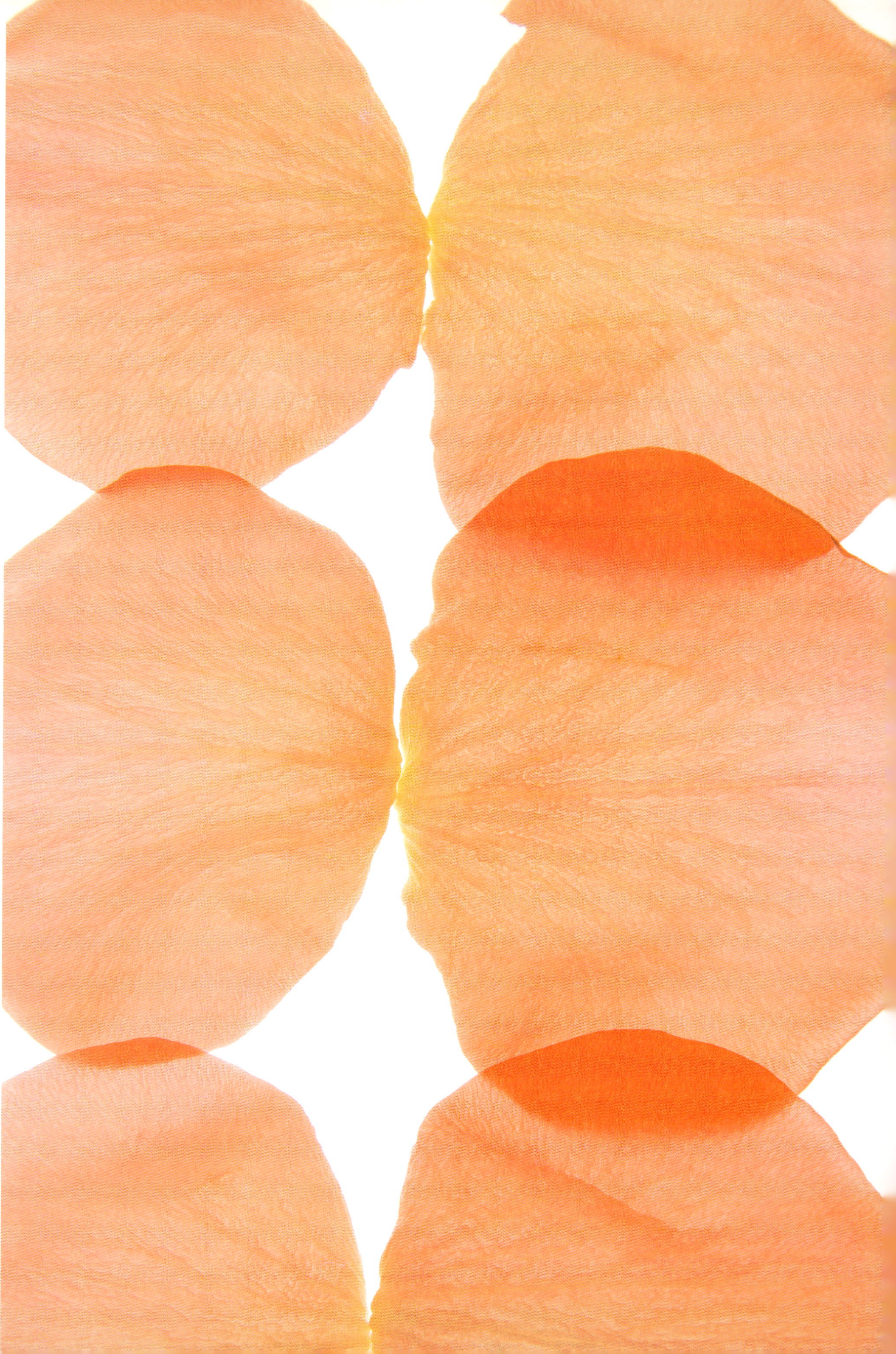

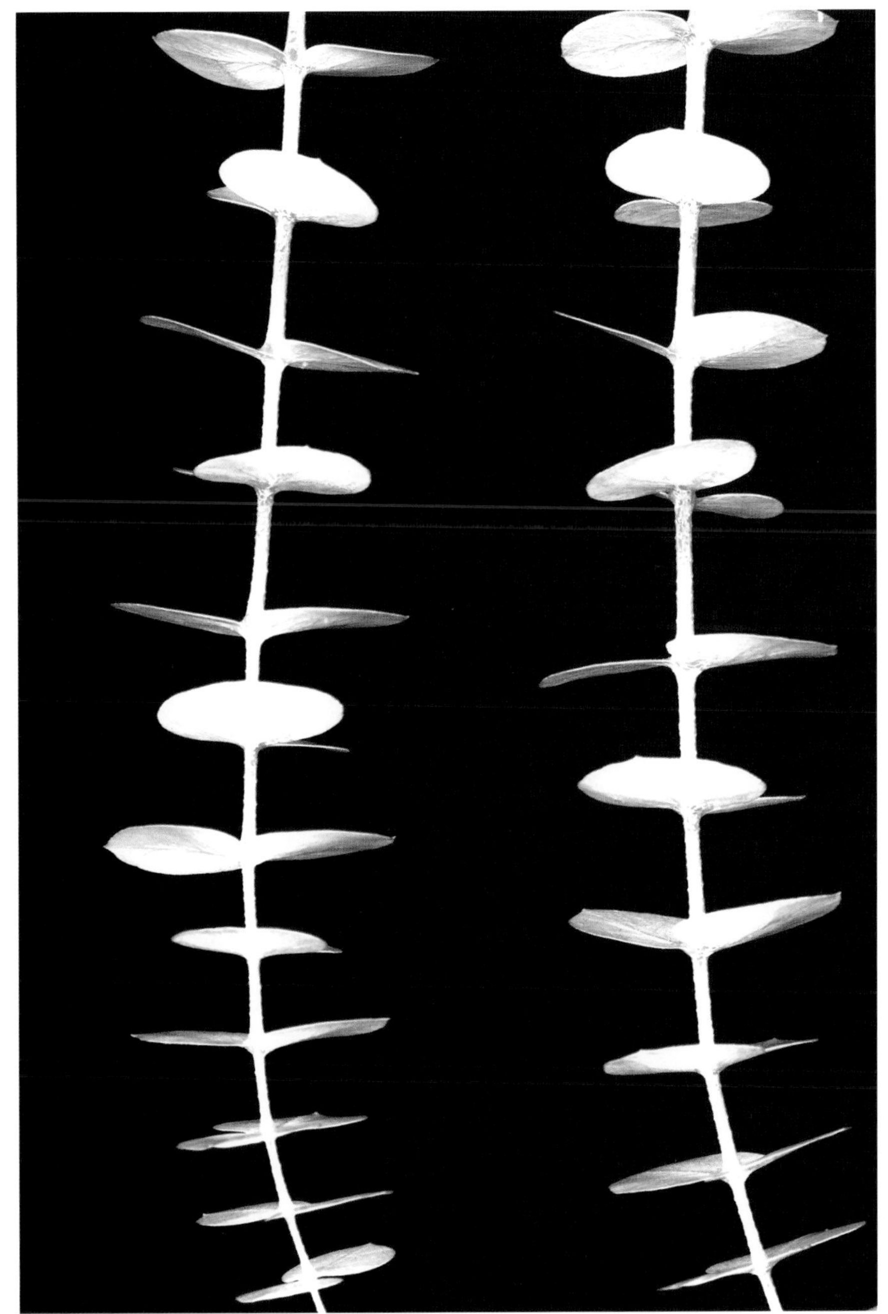

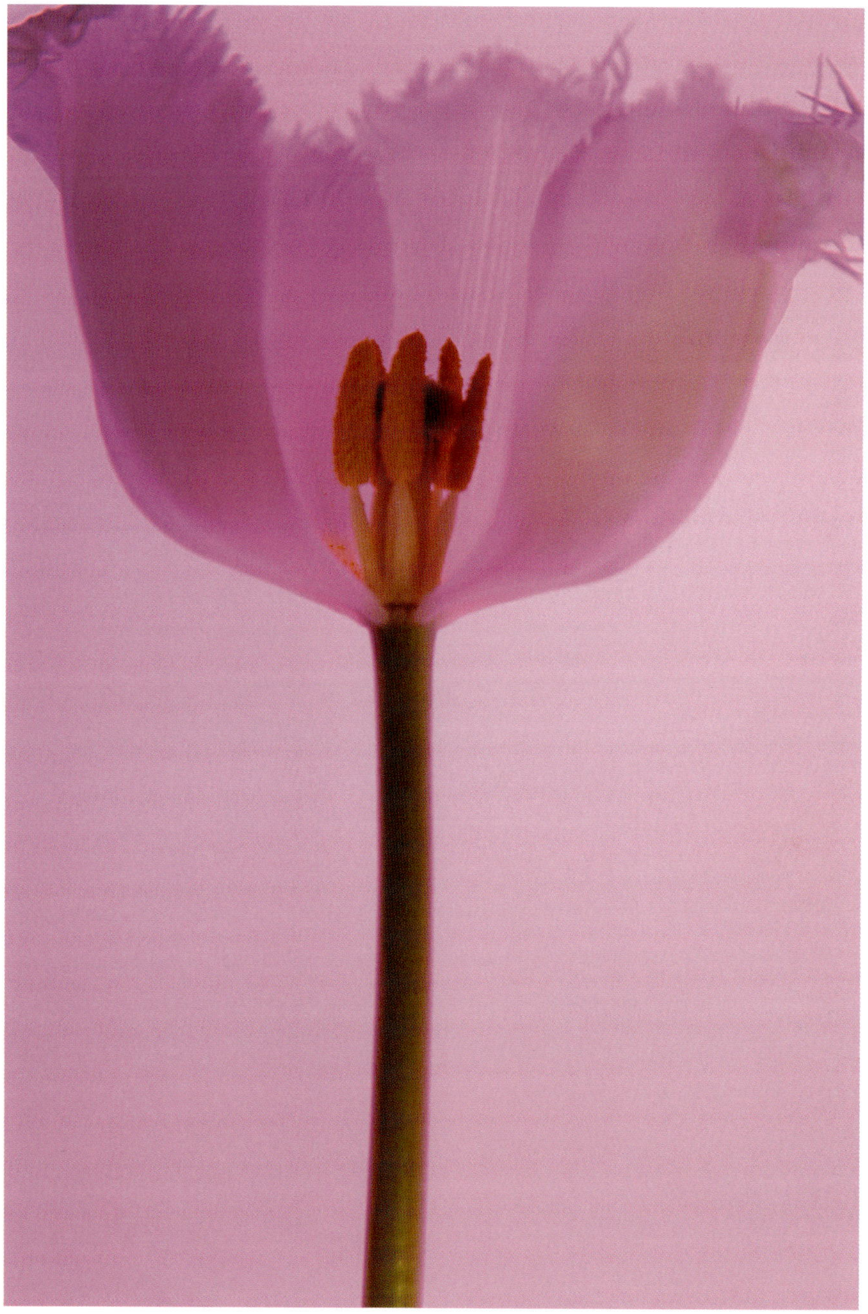

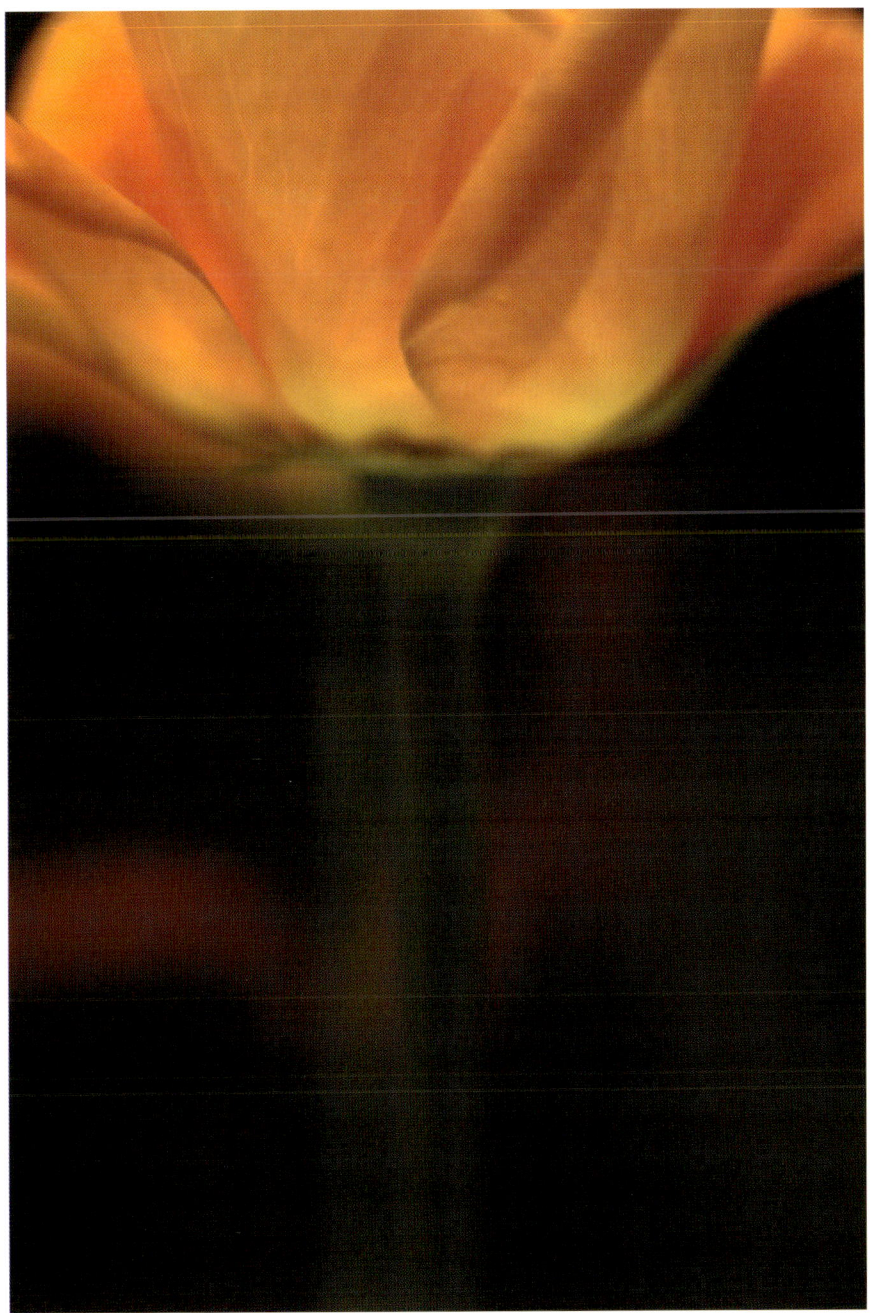

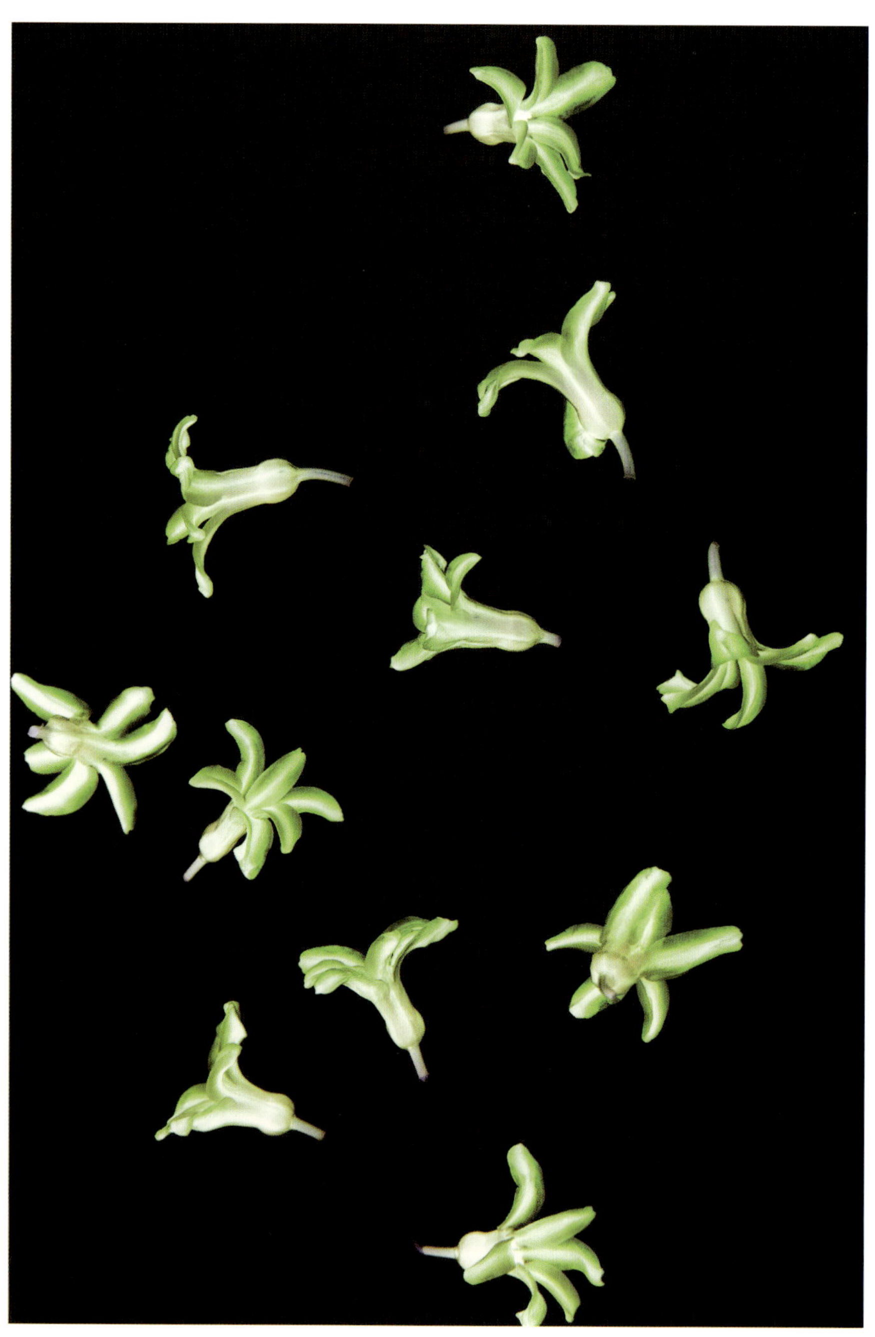

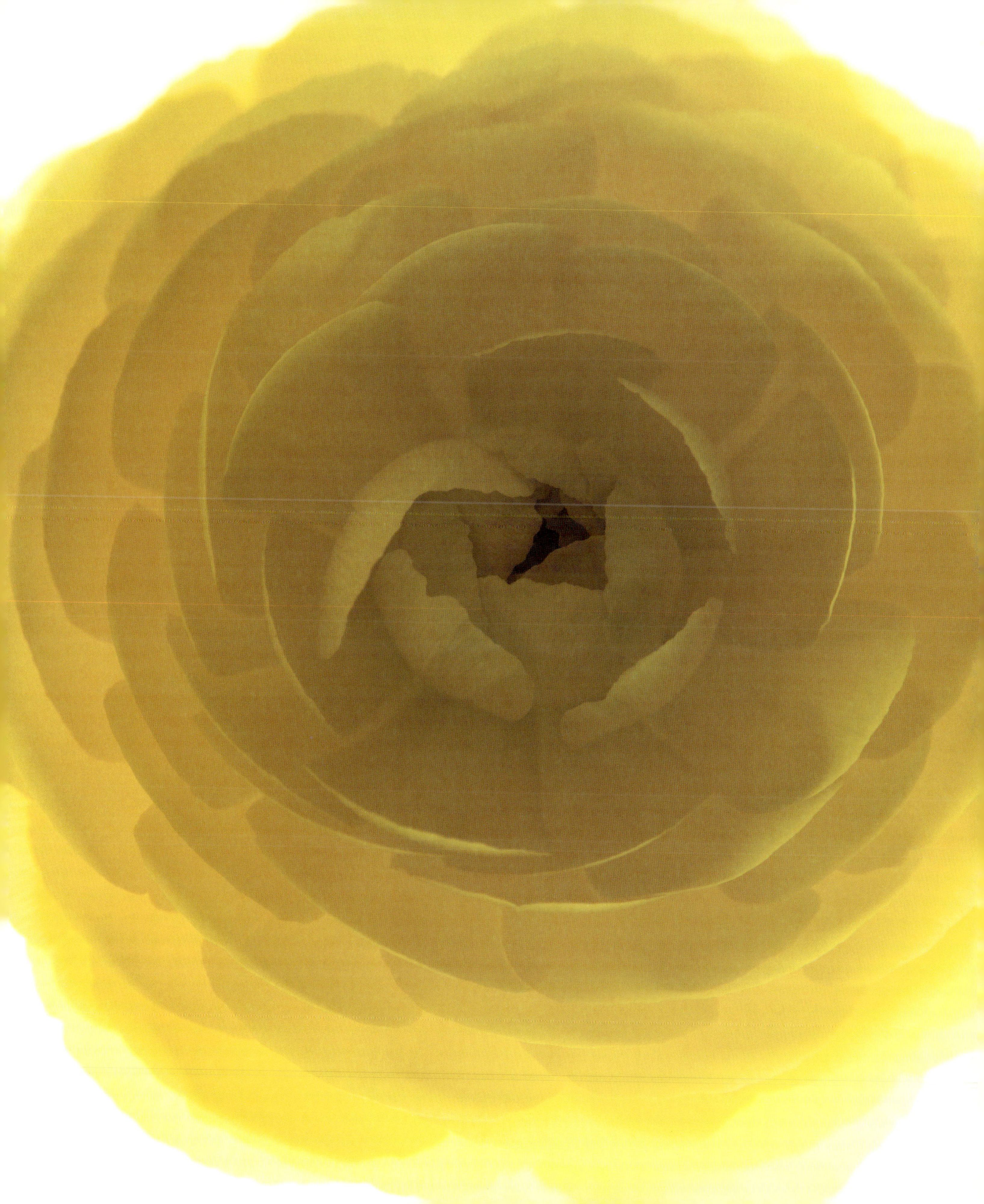

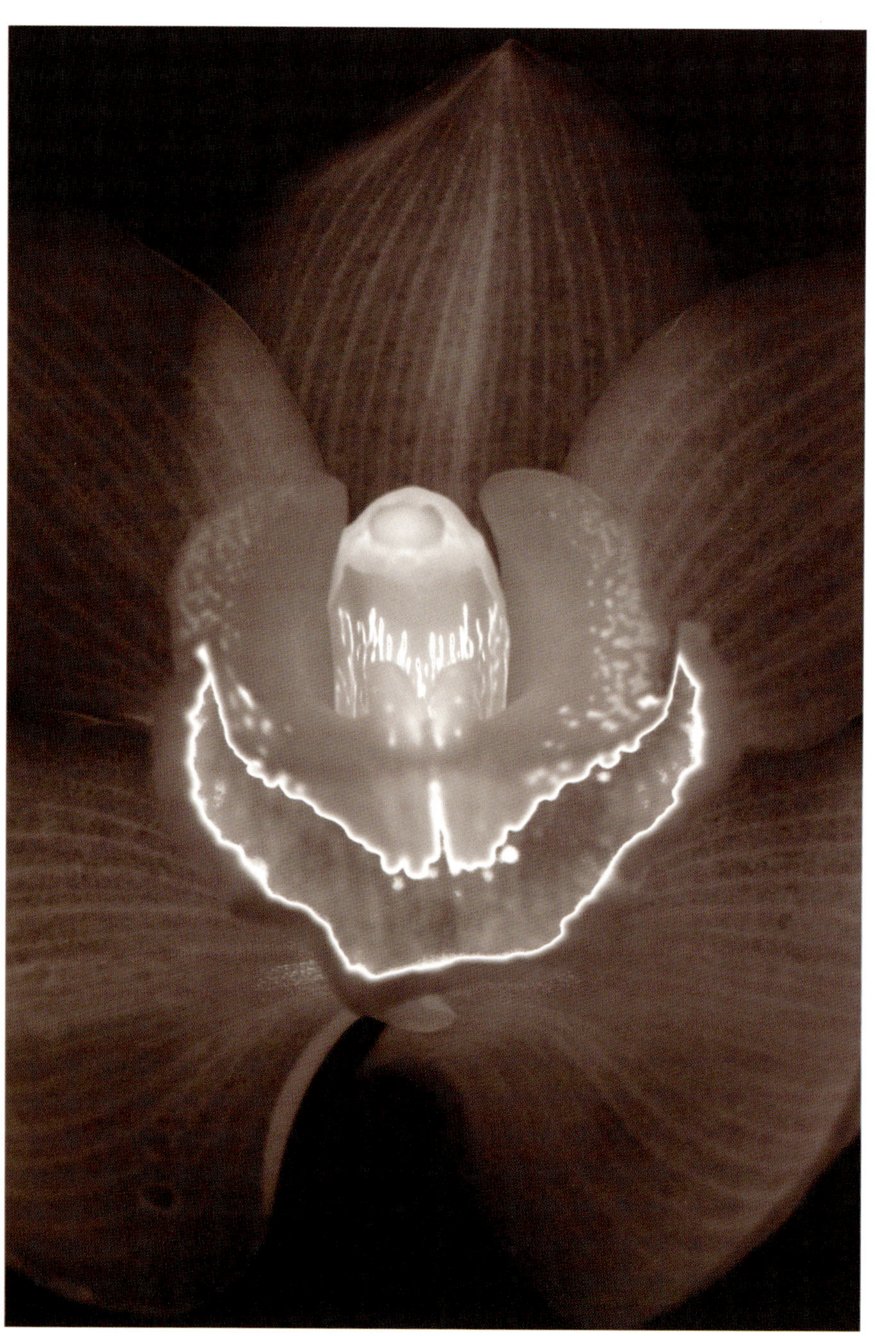

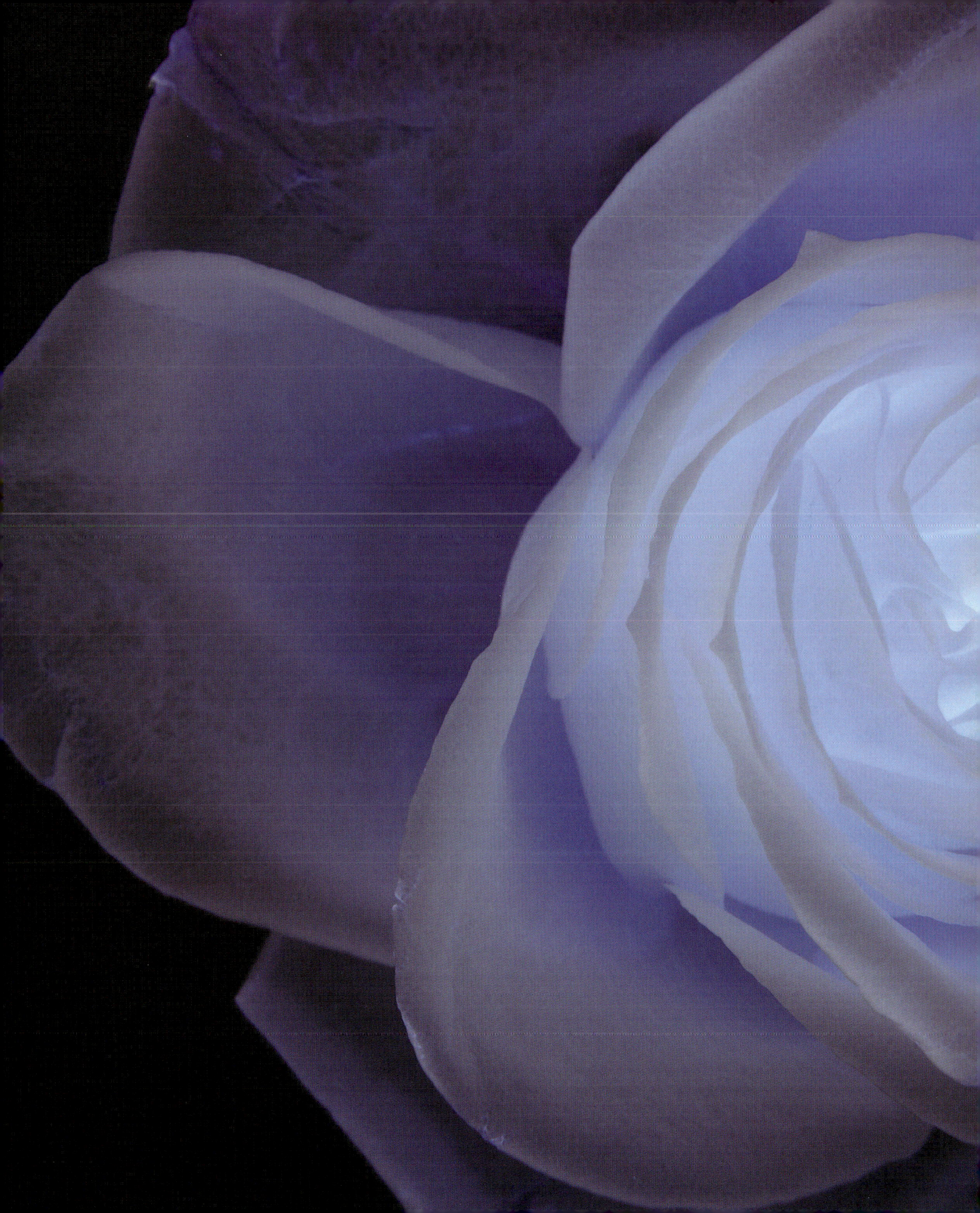

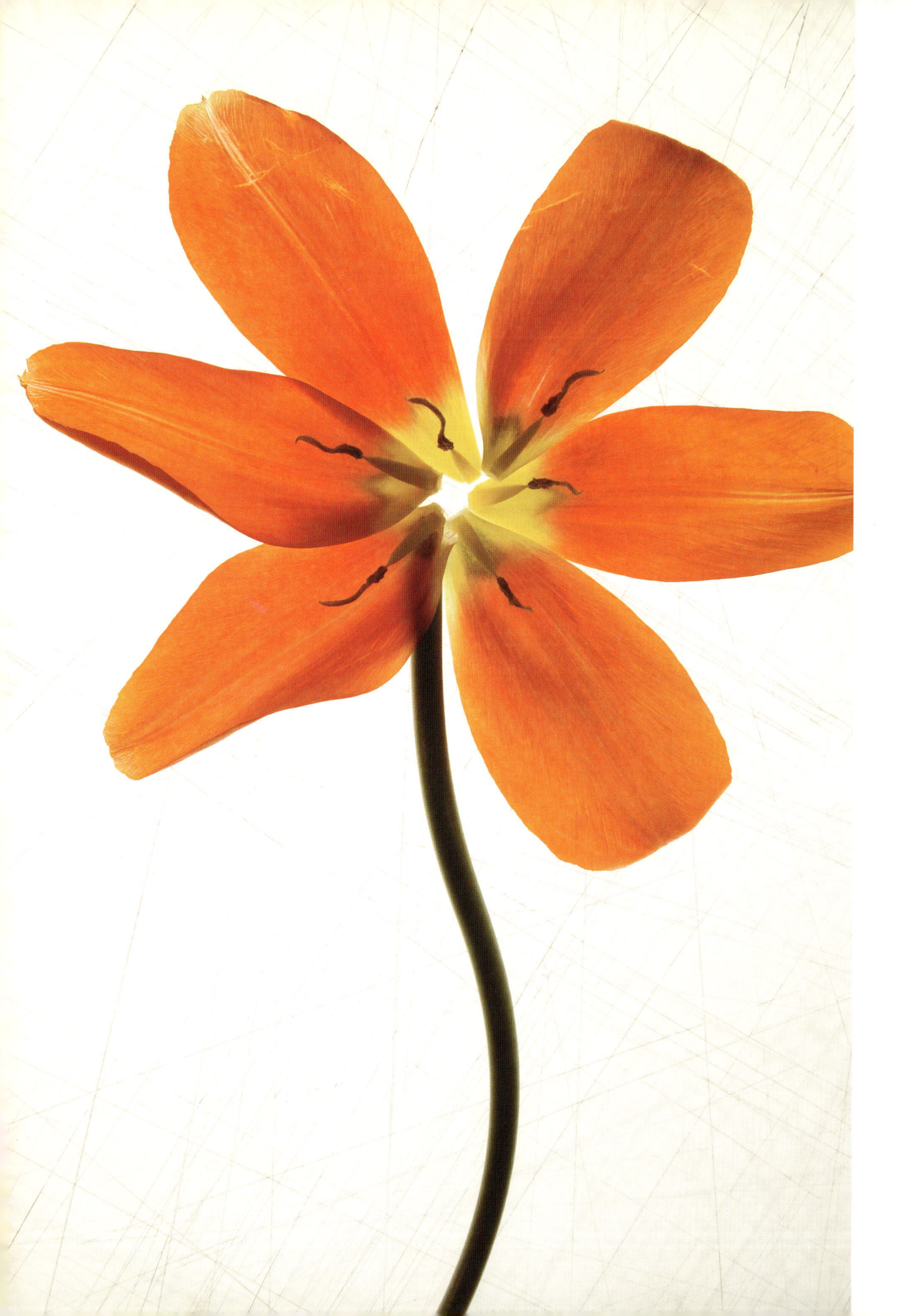

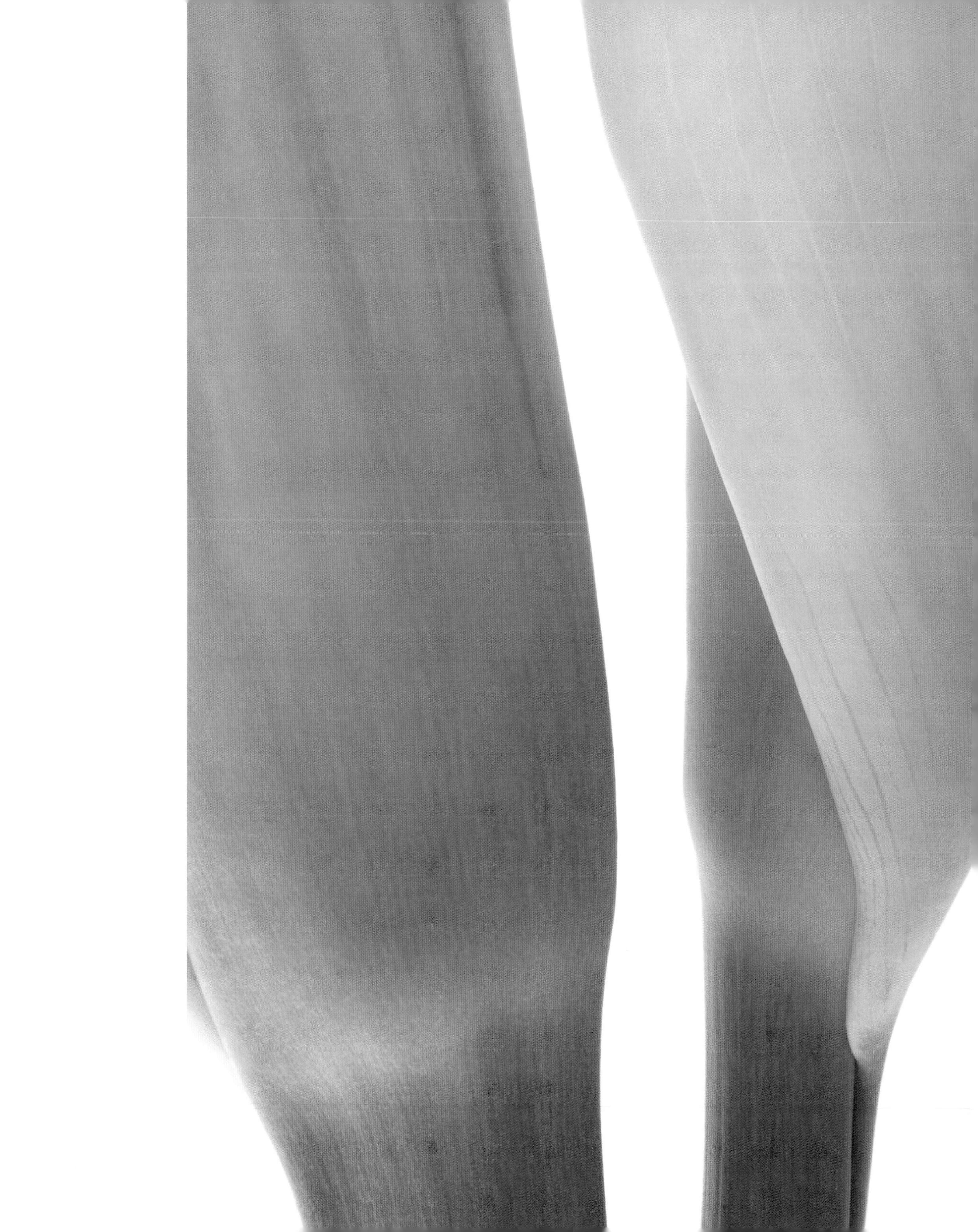

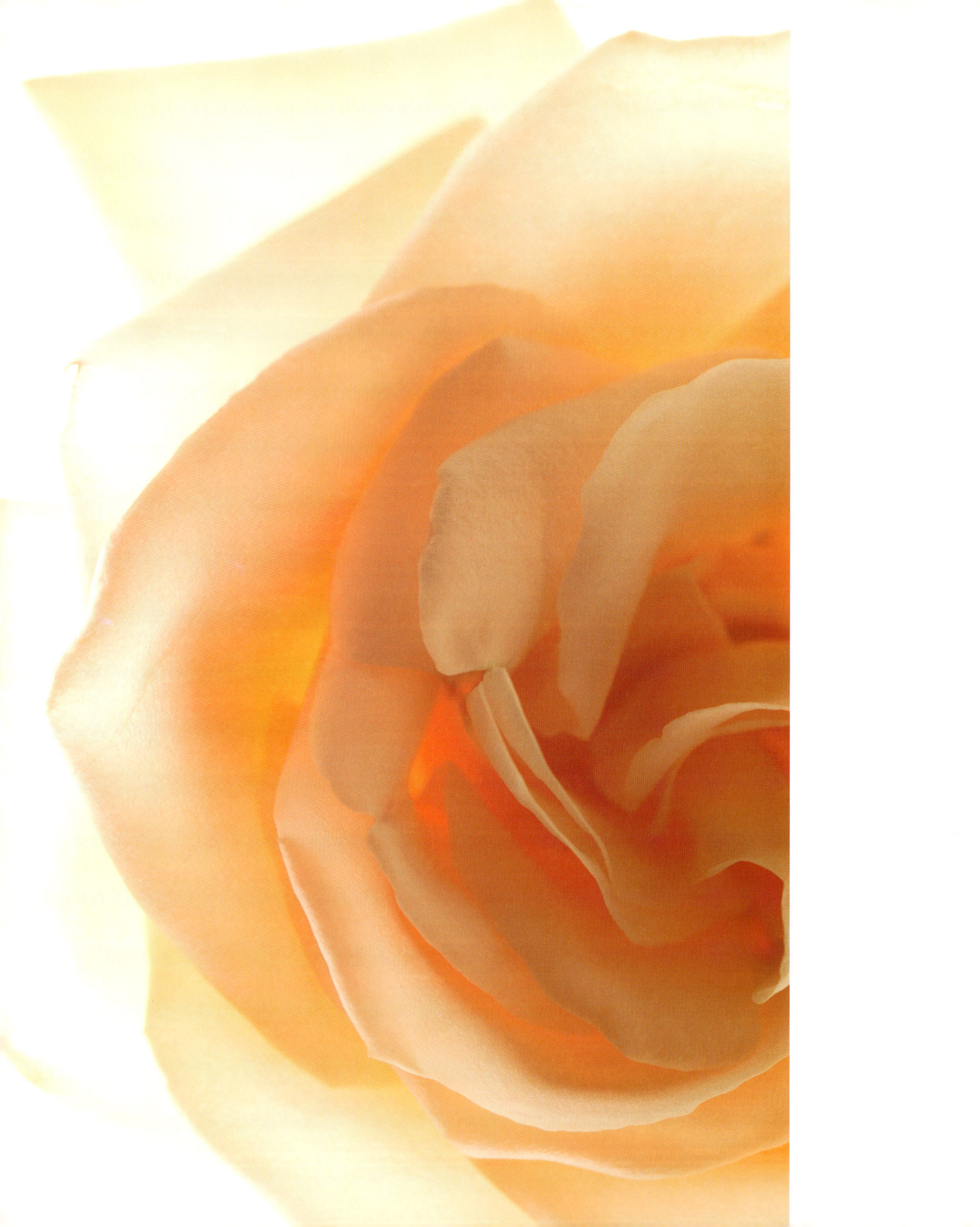

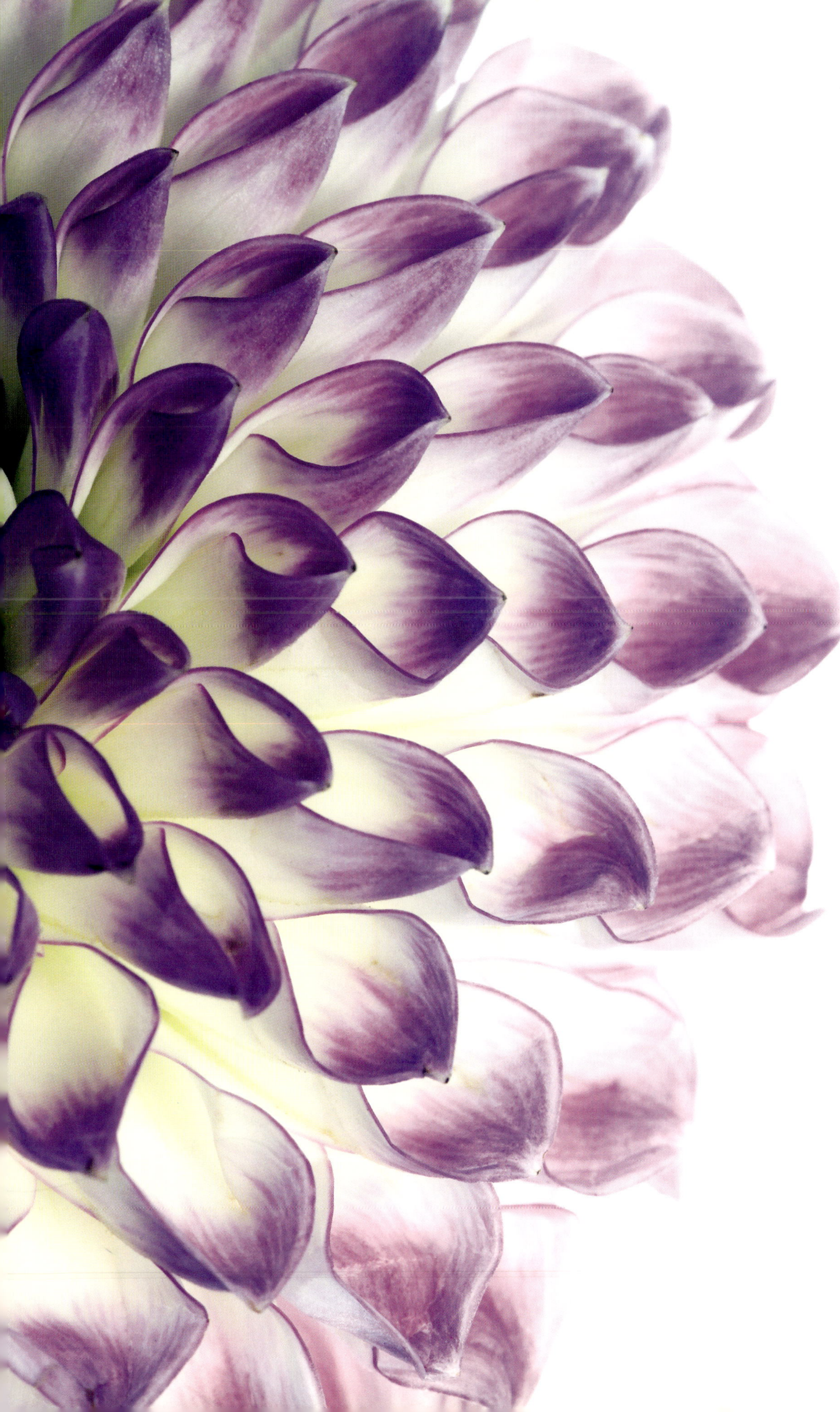

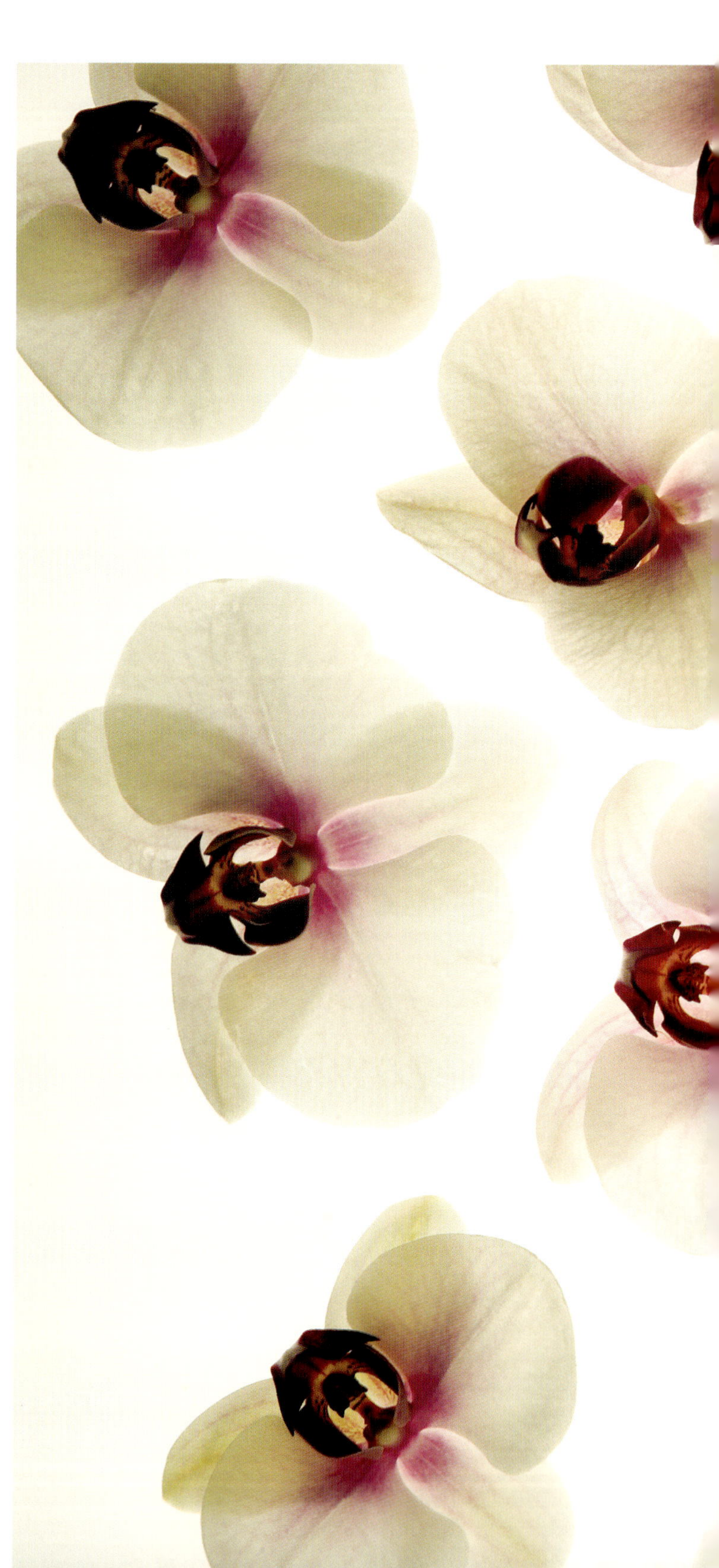

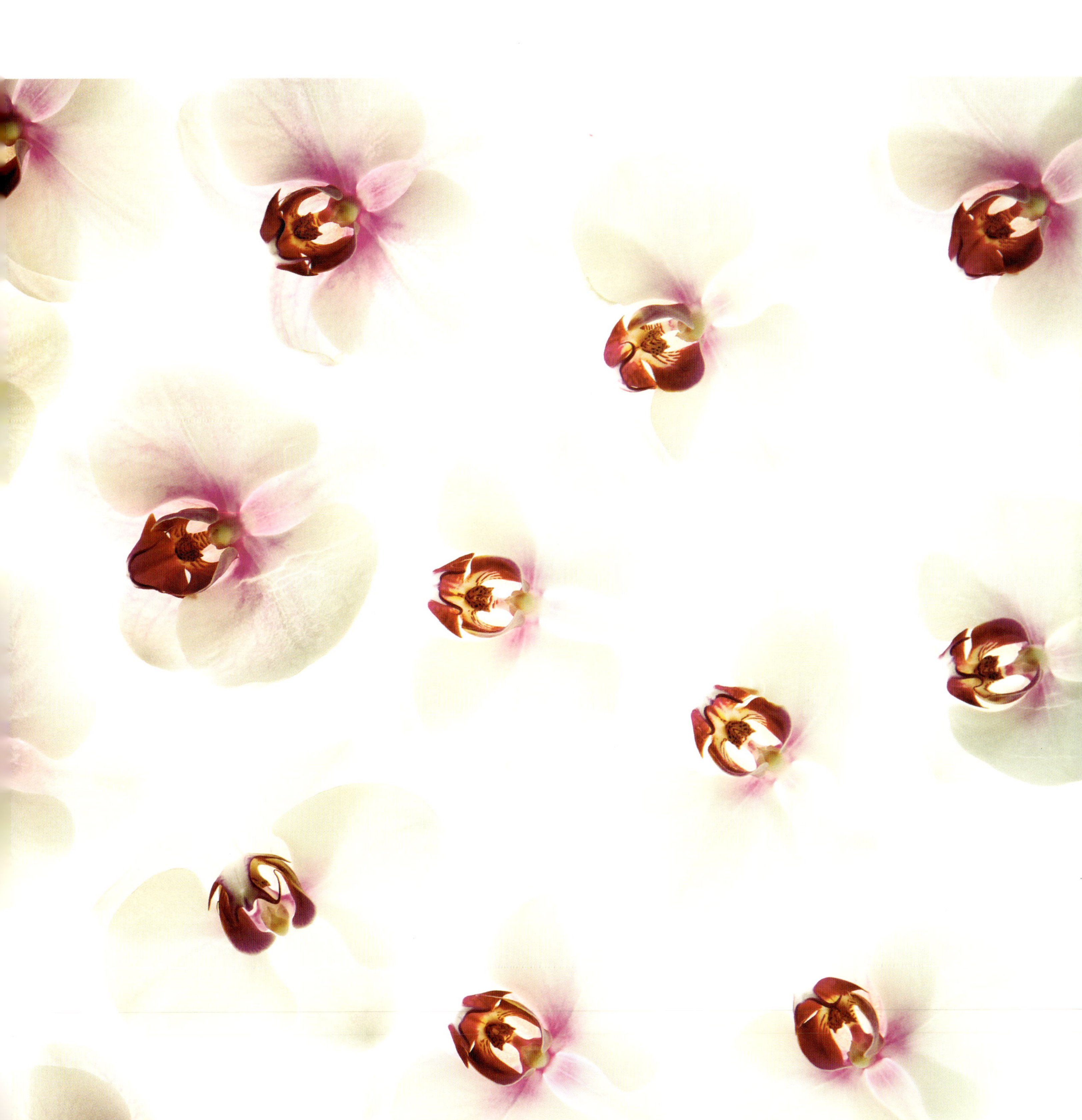

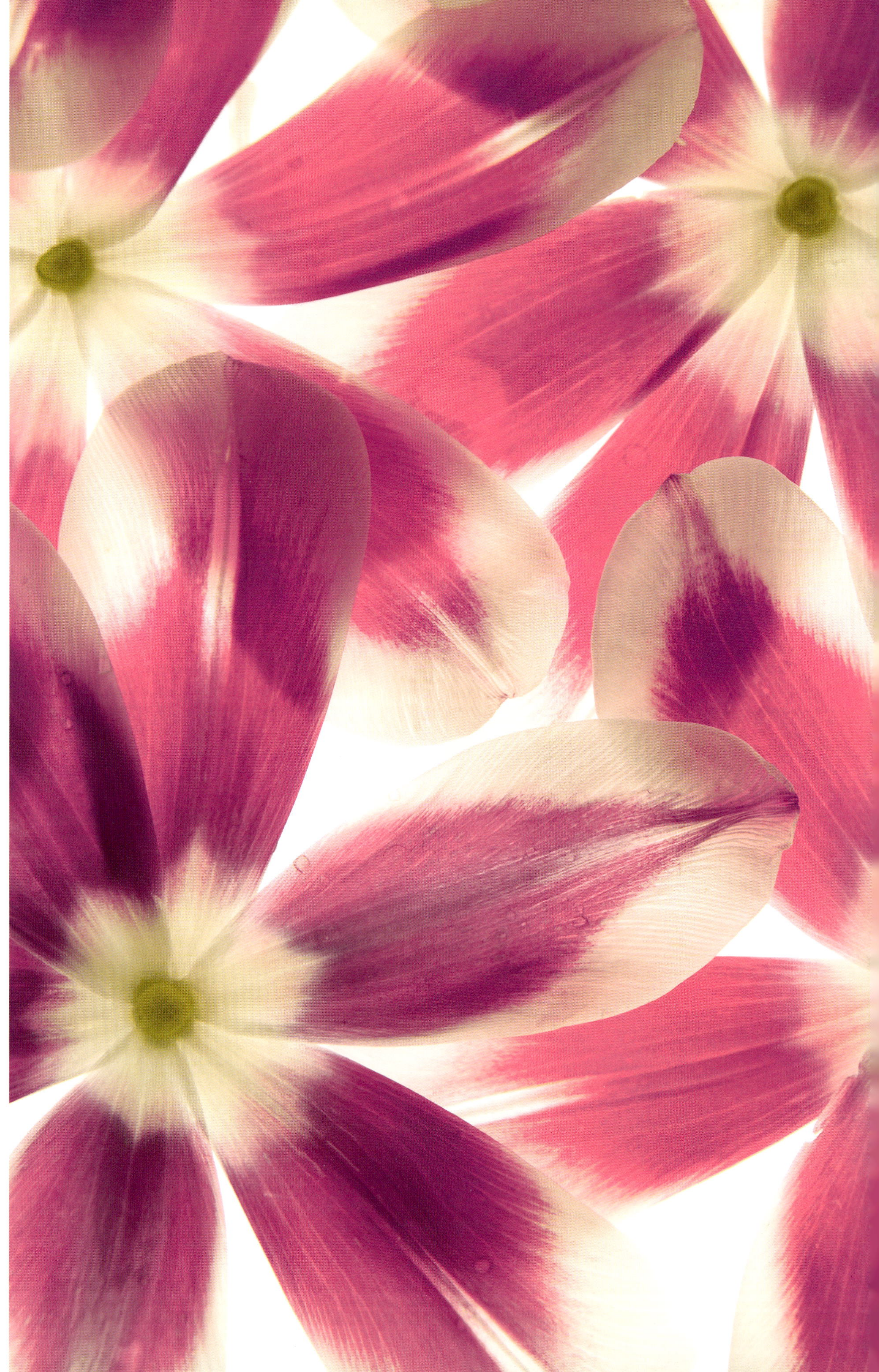

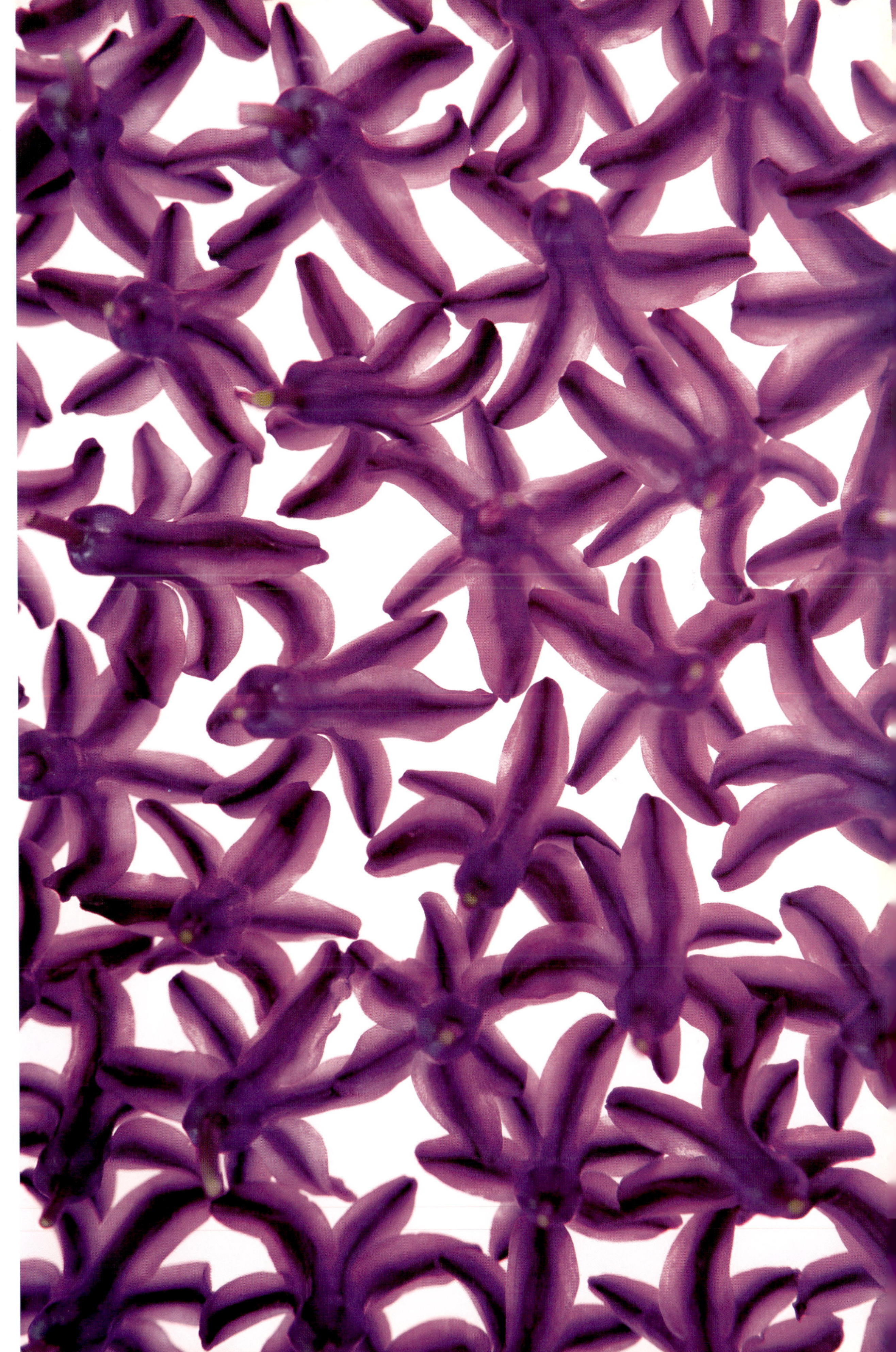

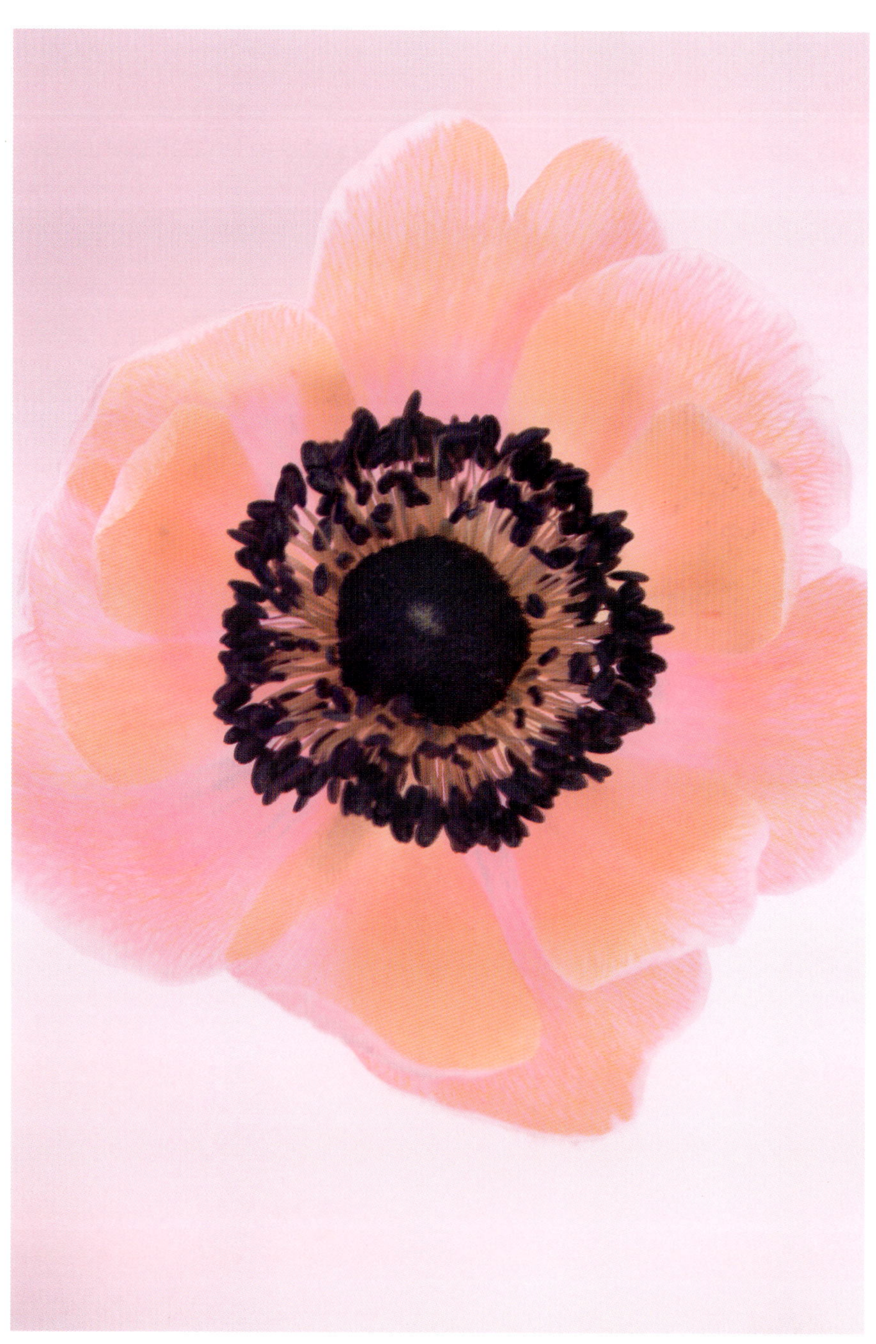

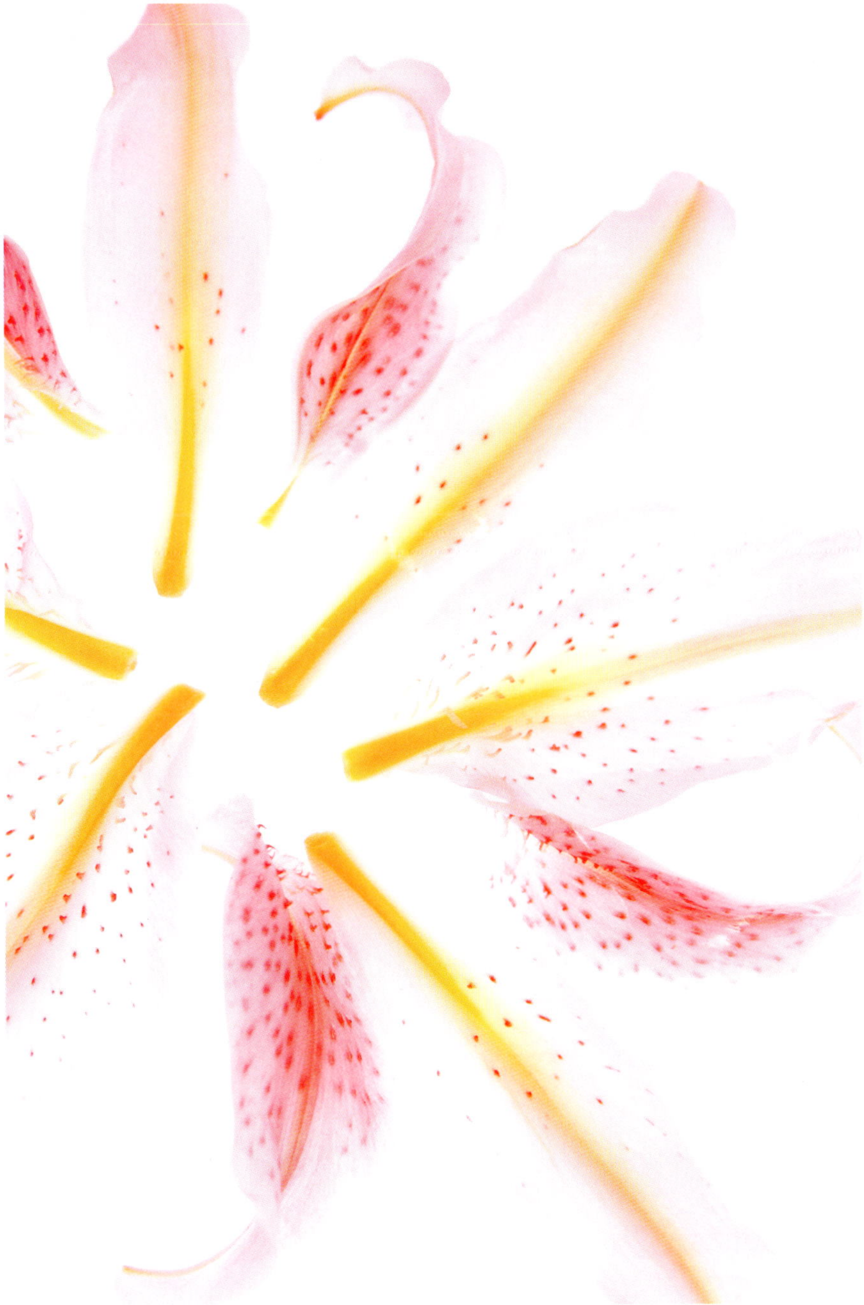

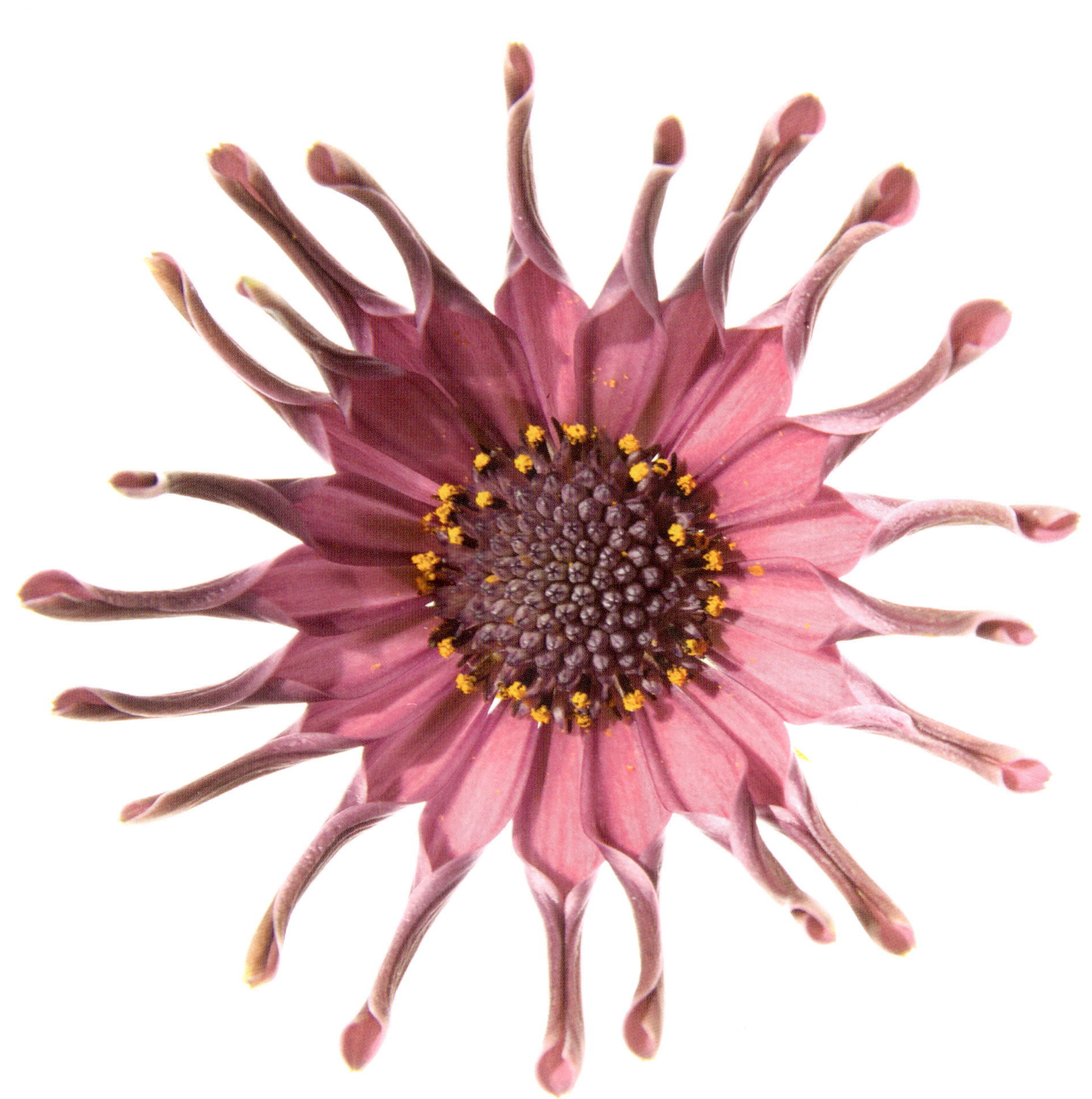

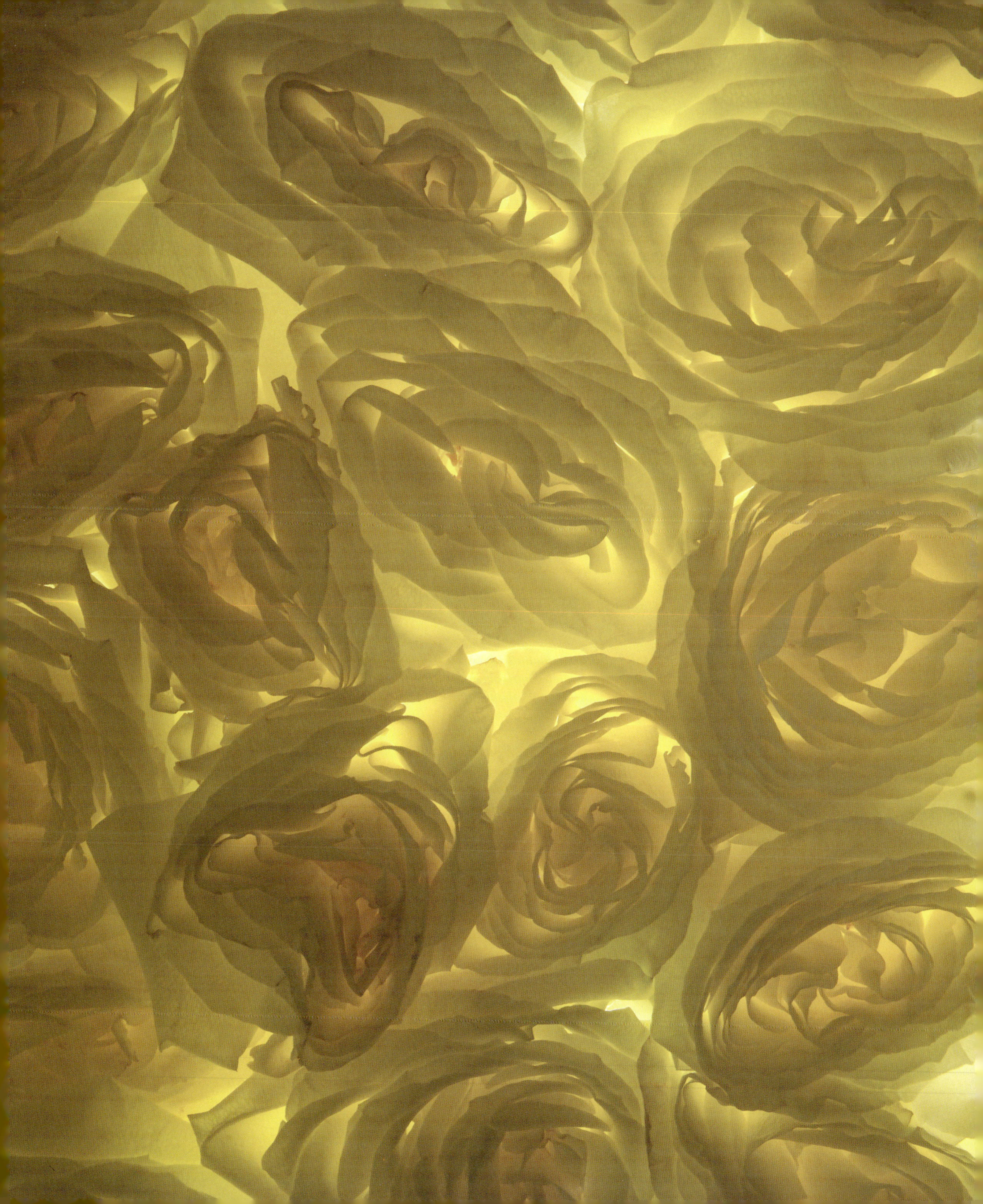

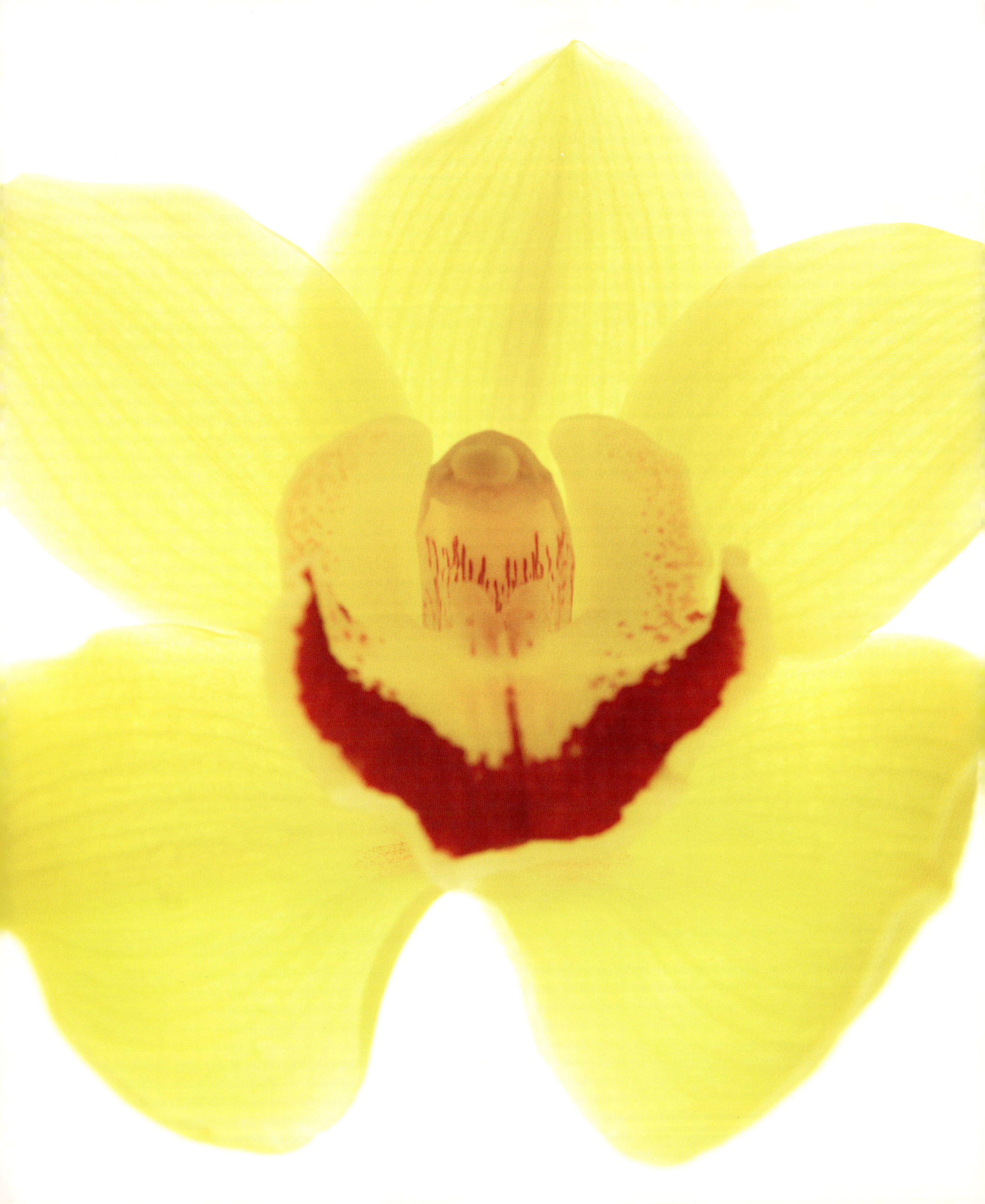

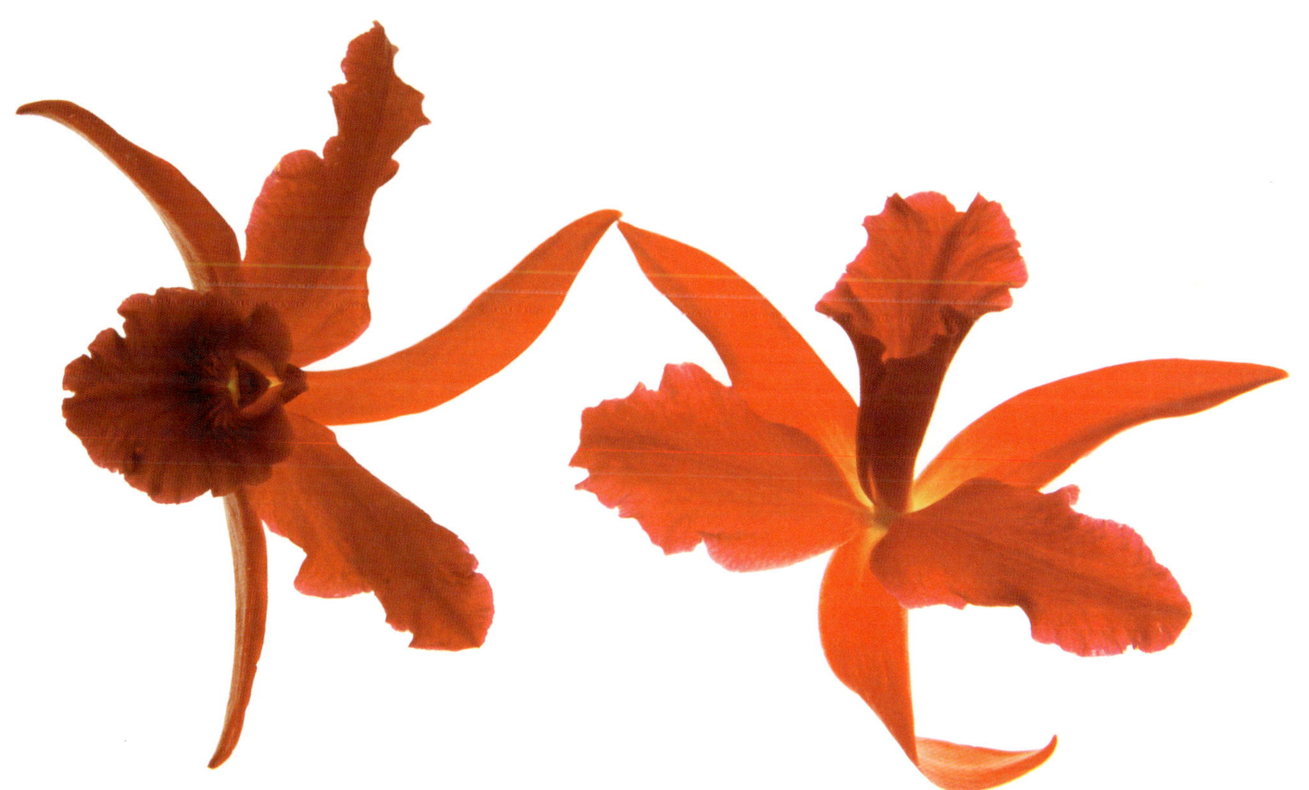

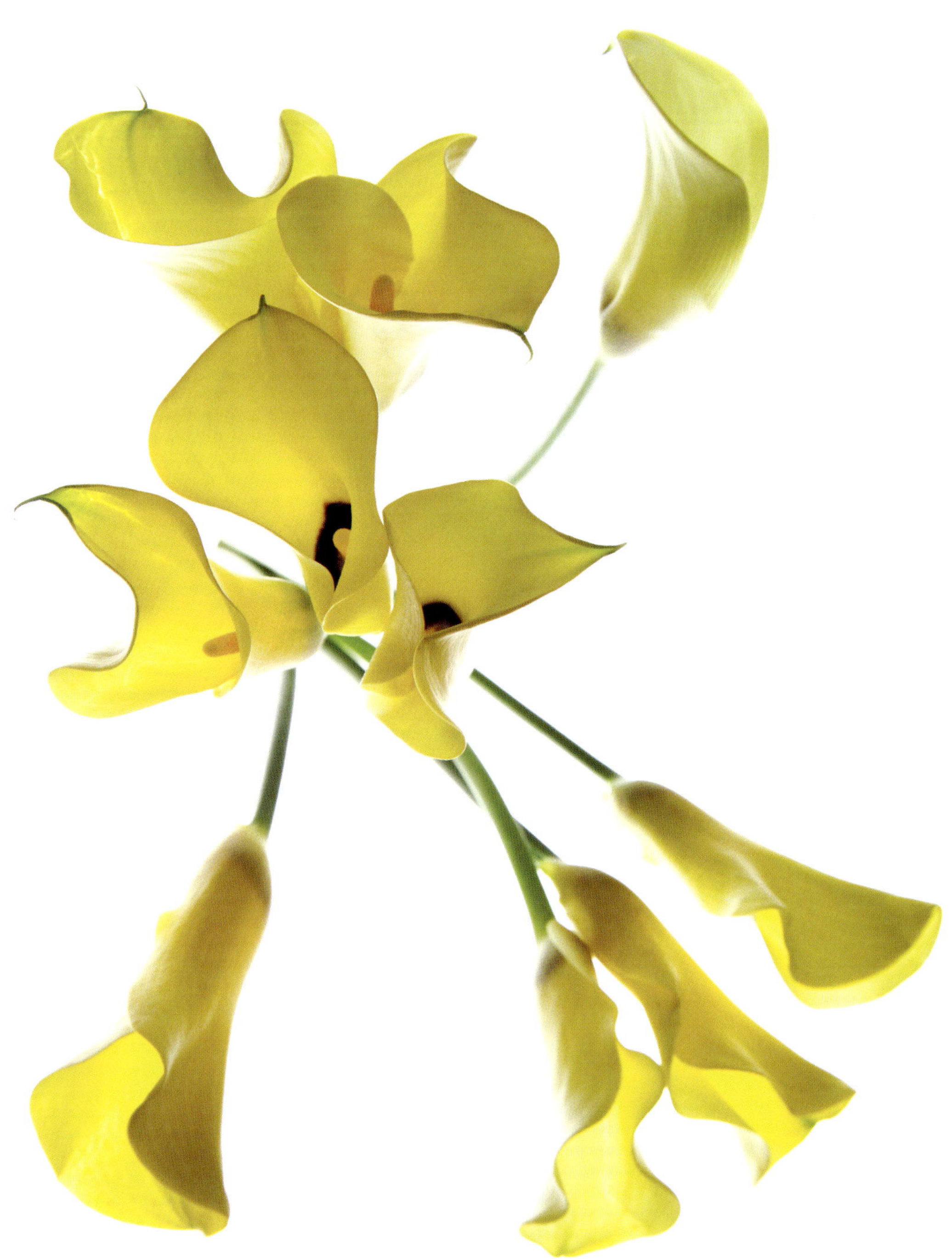

P44

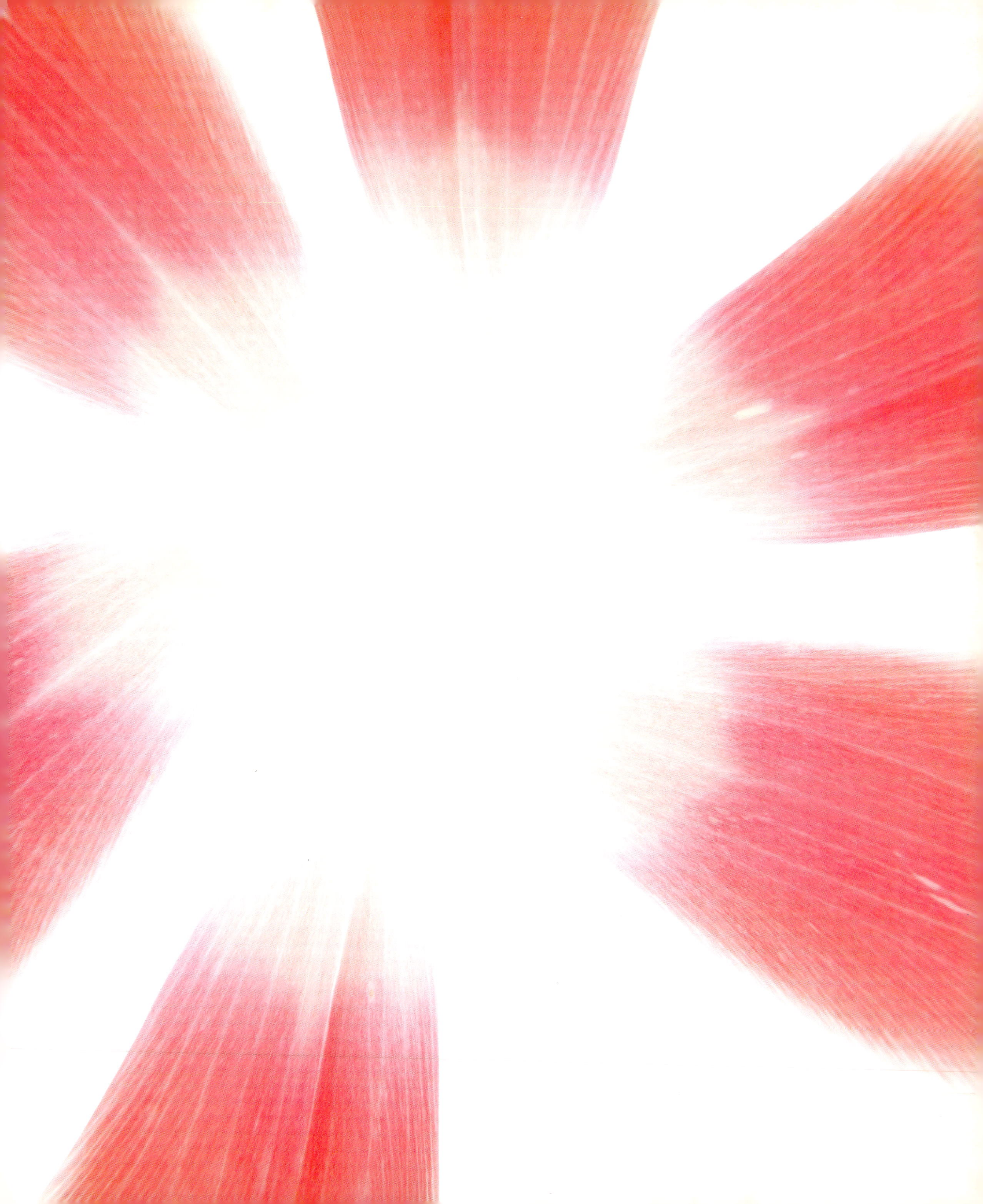

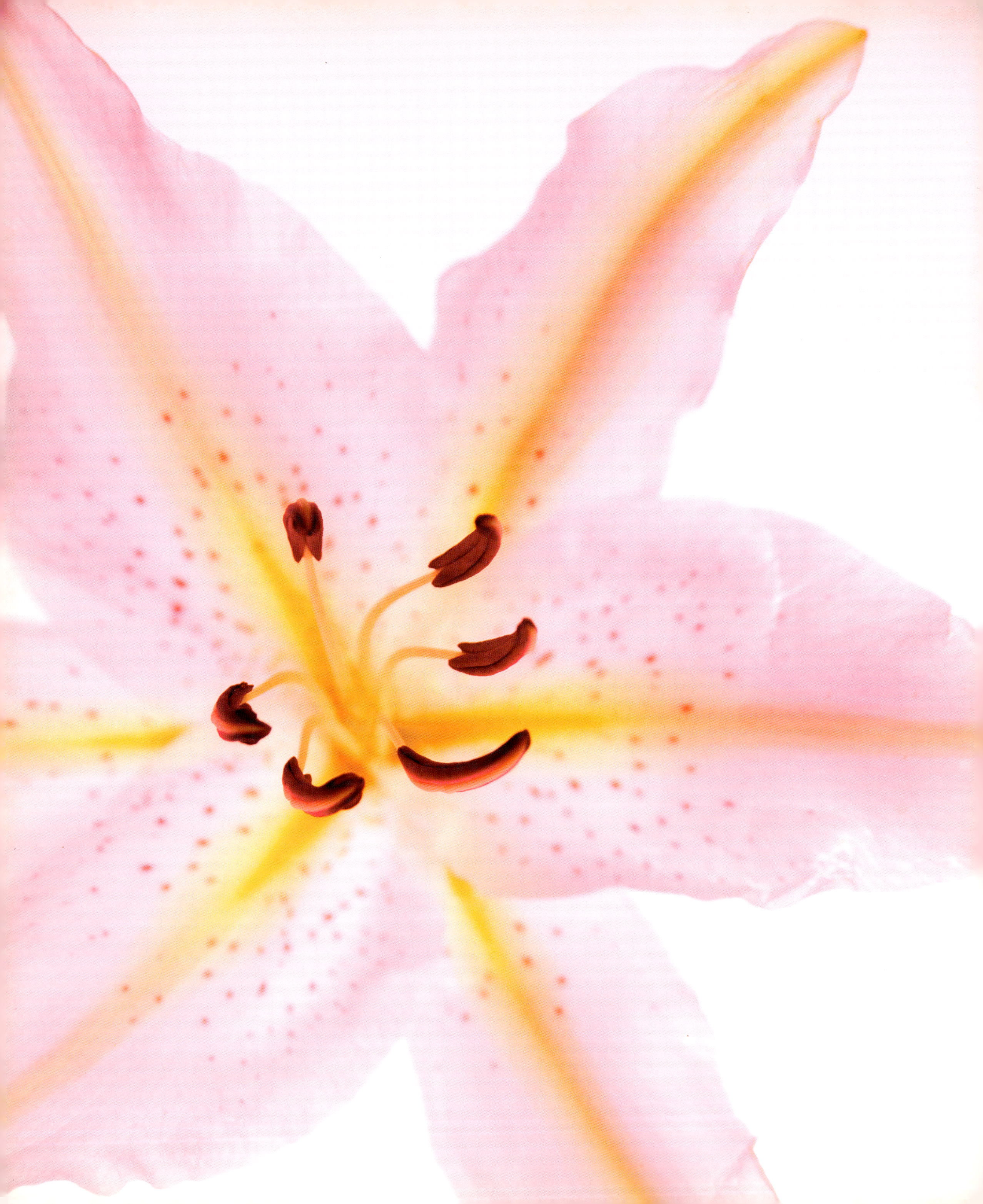

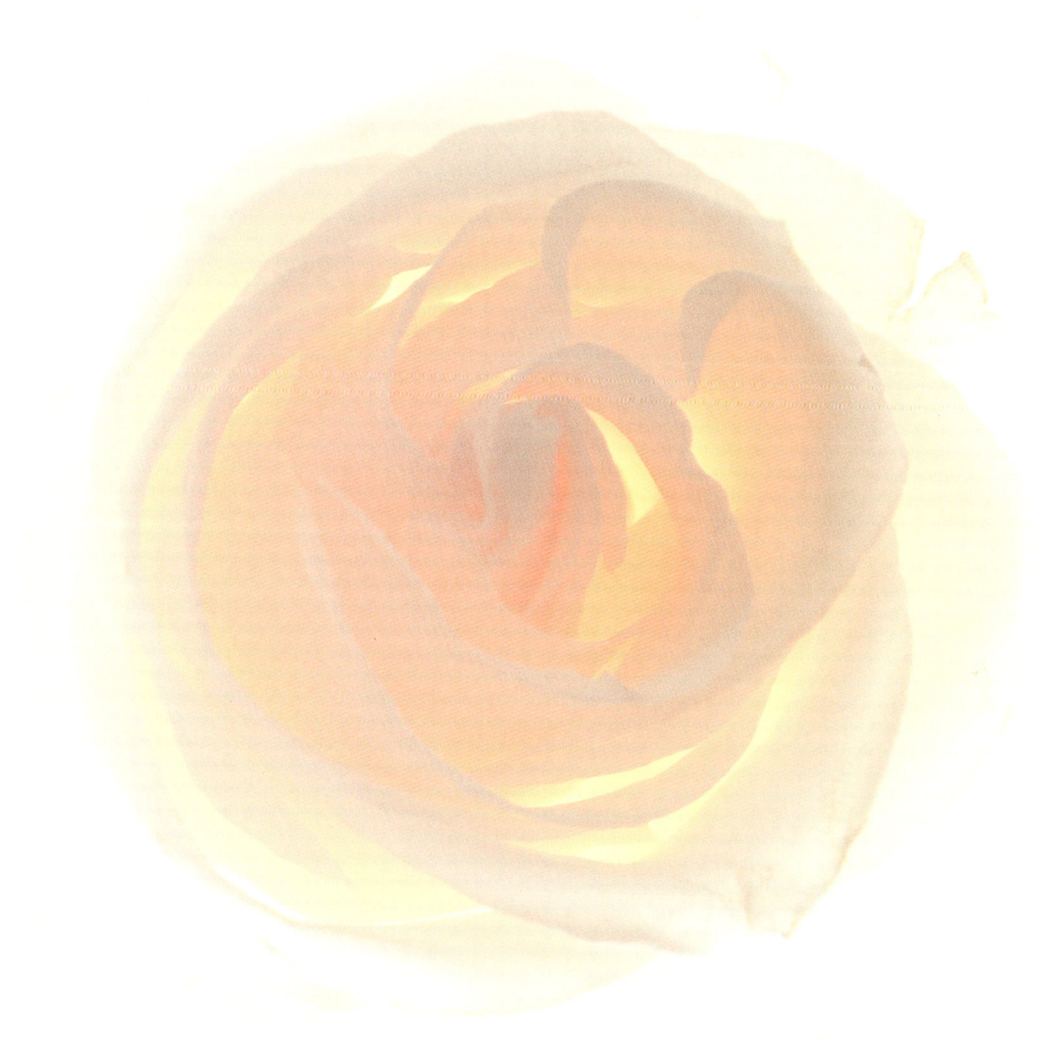

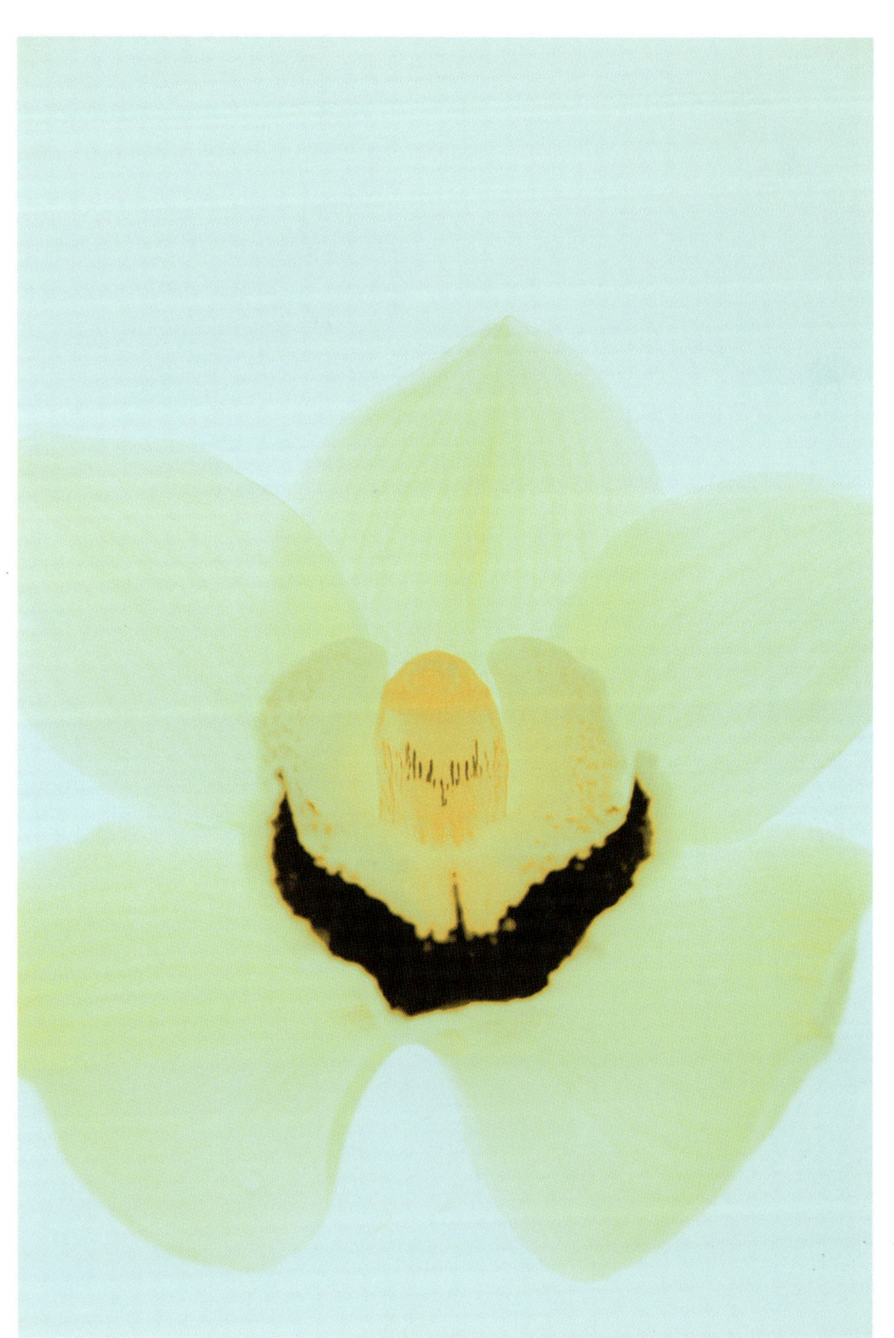

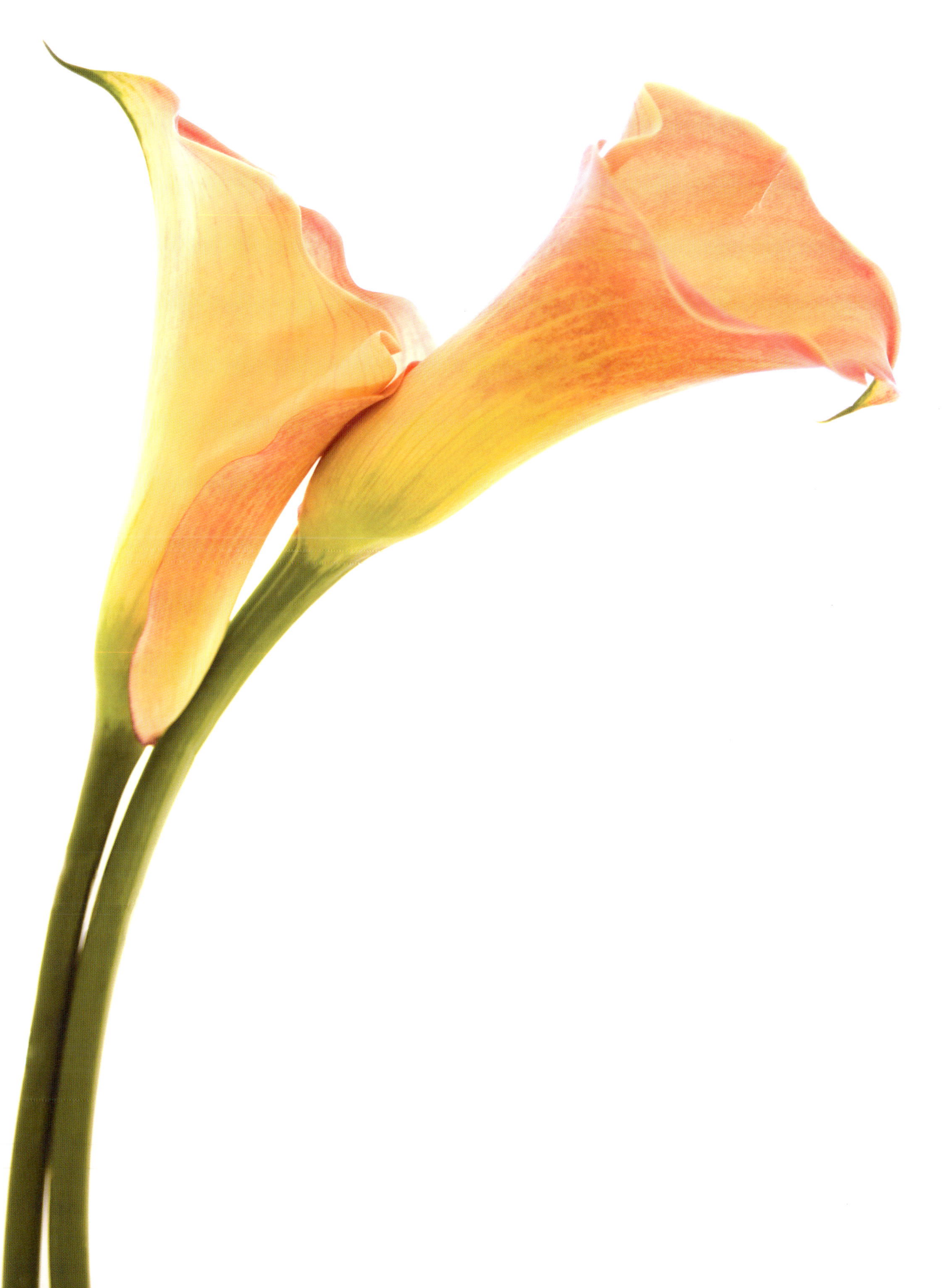

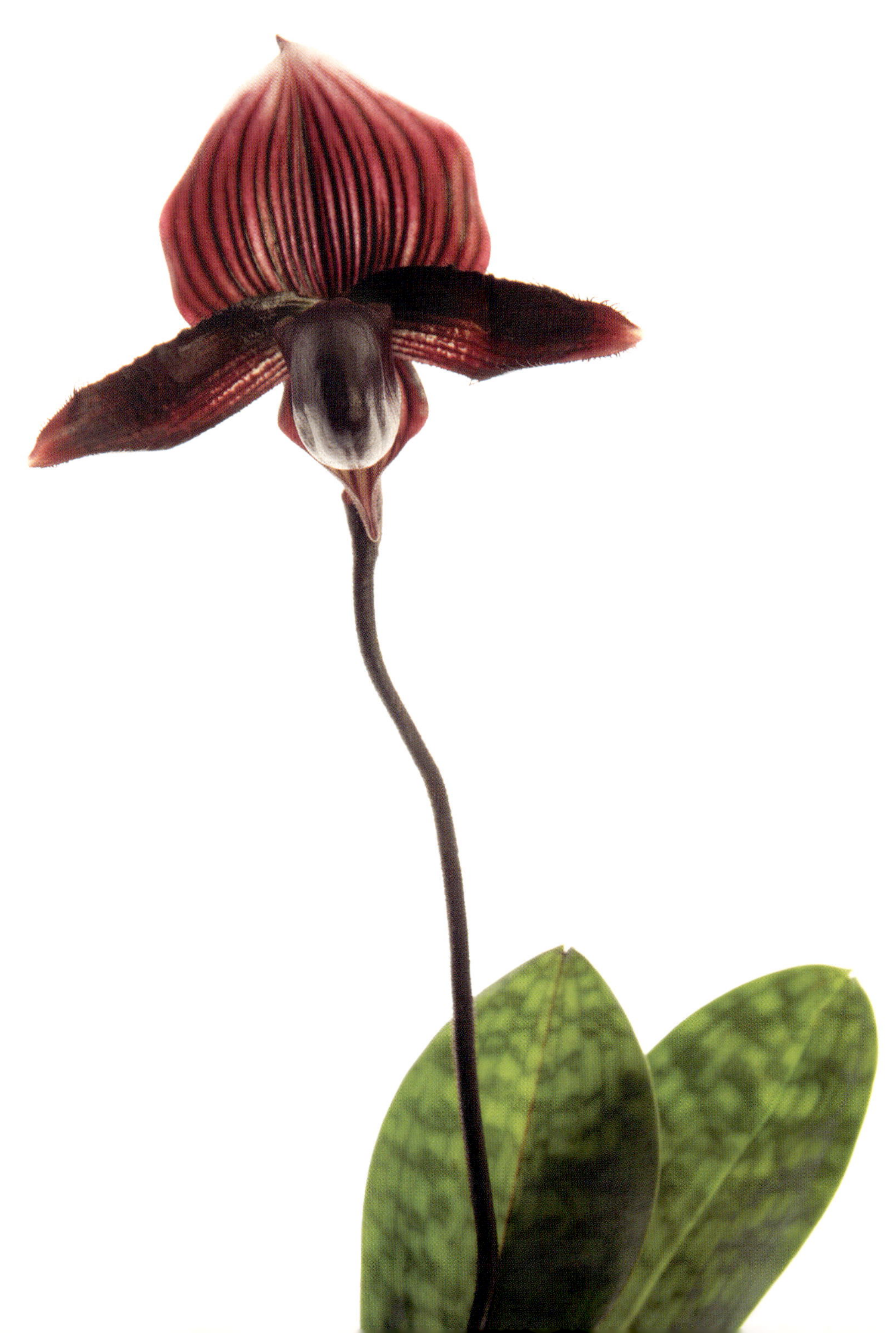

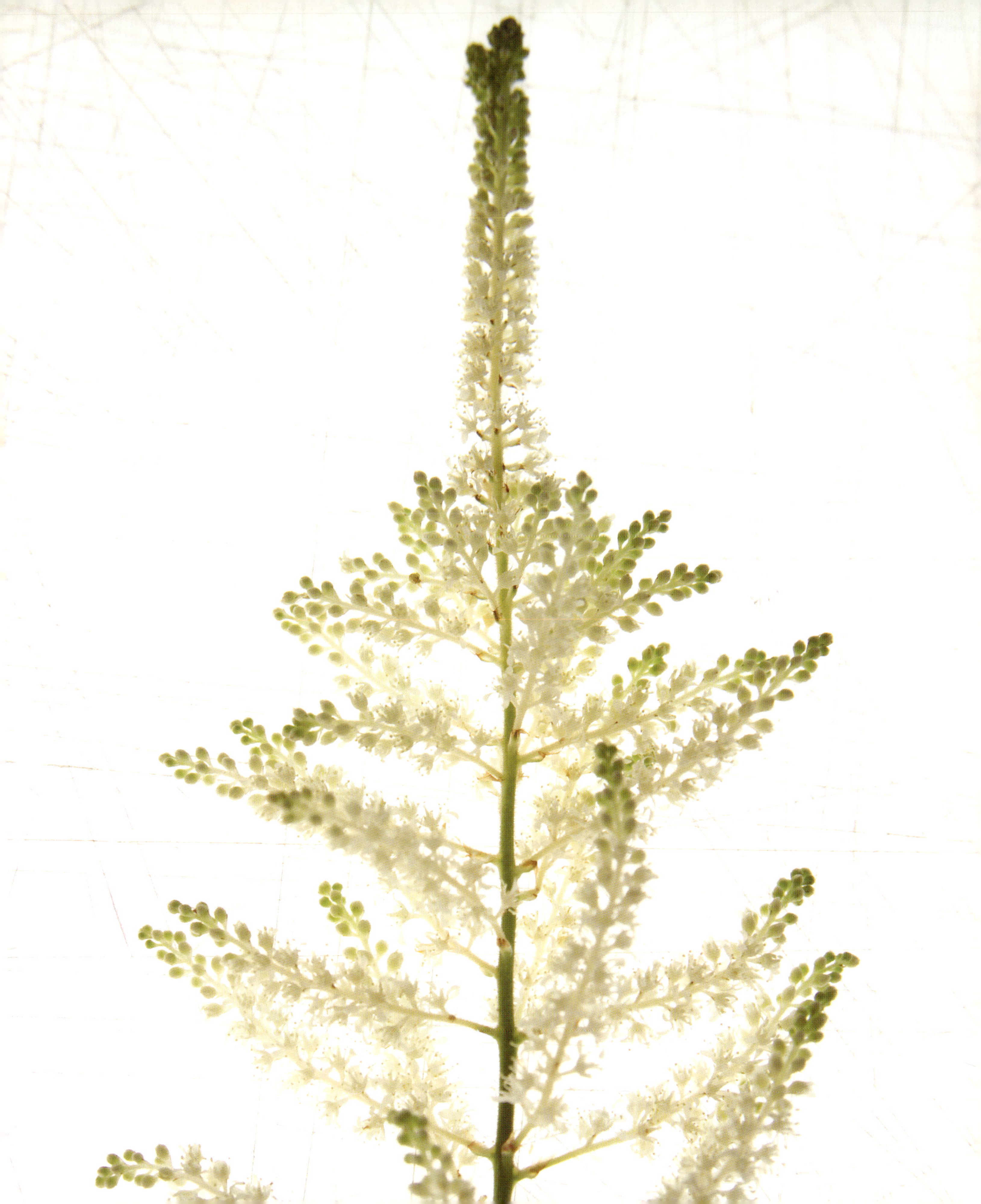

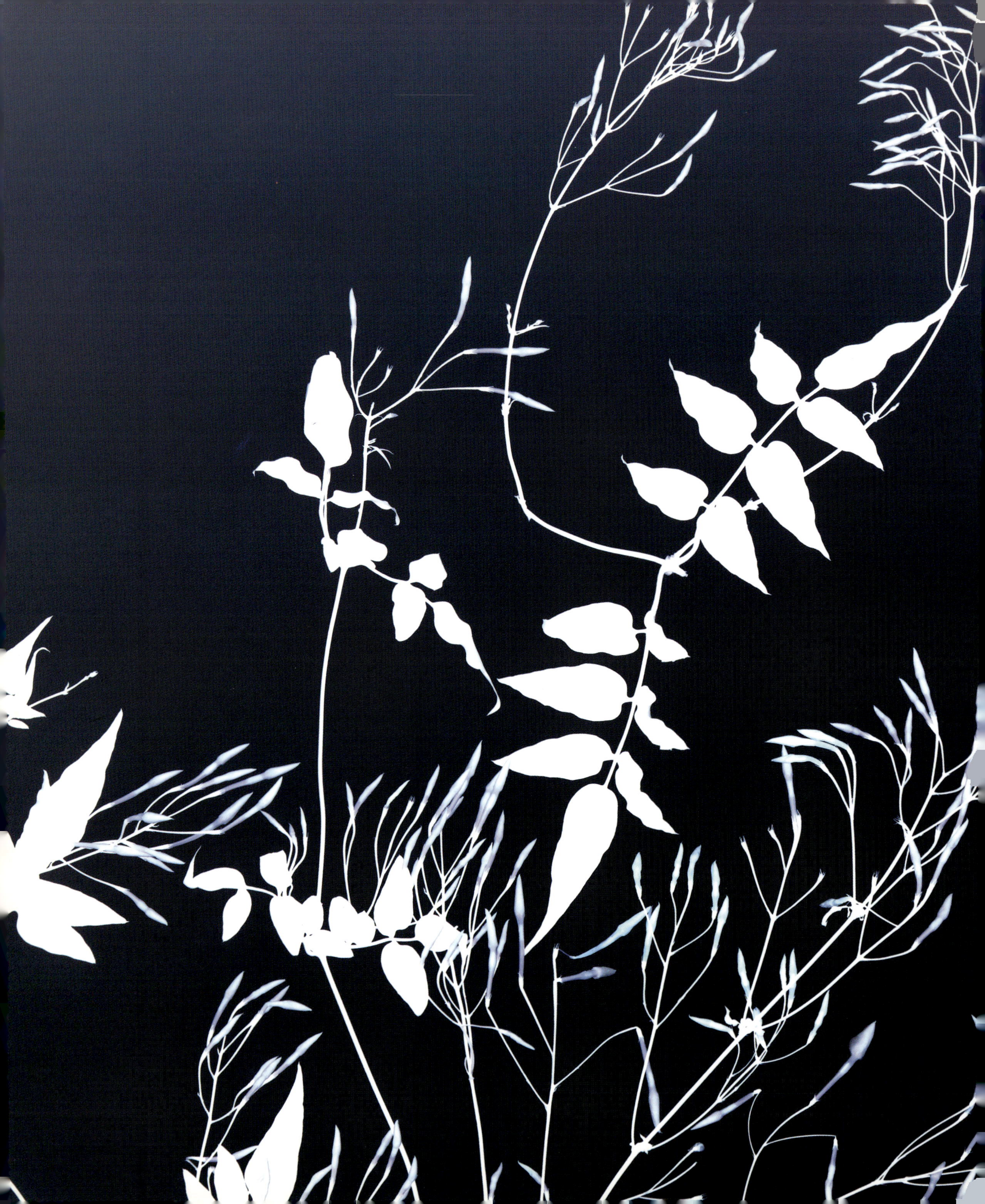

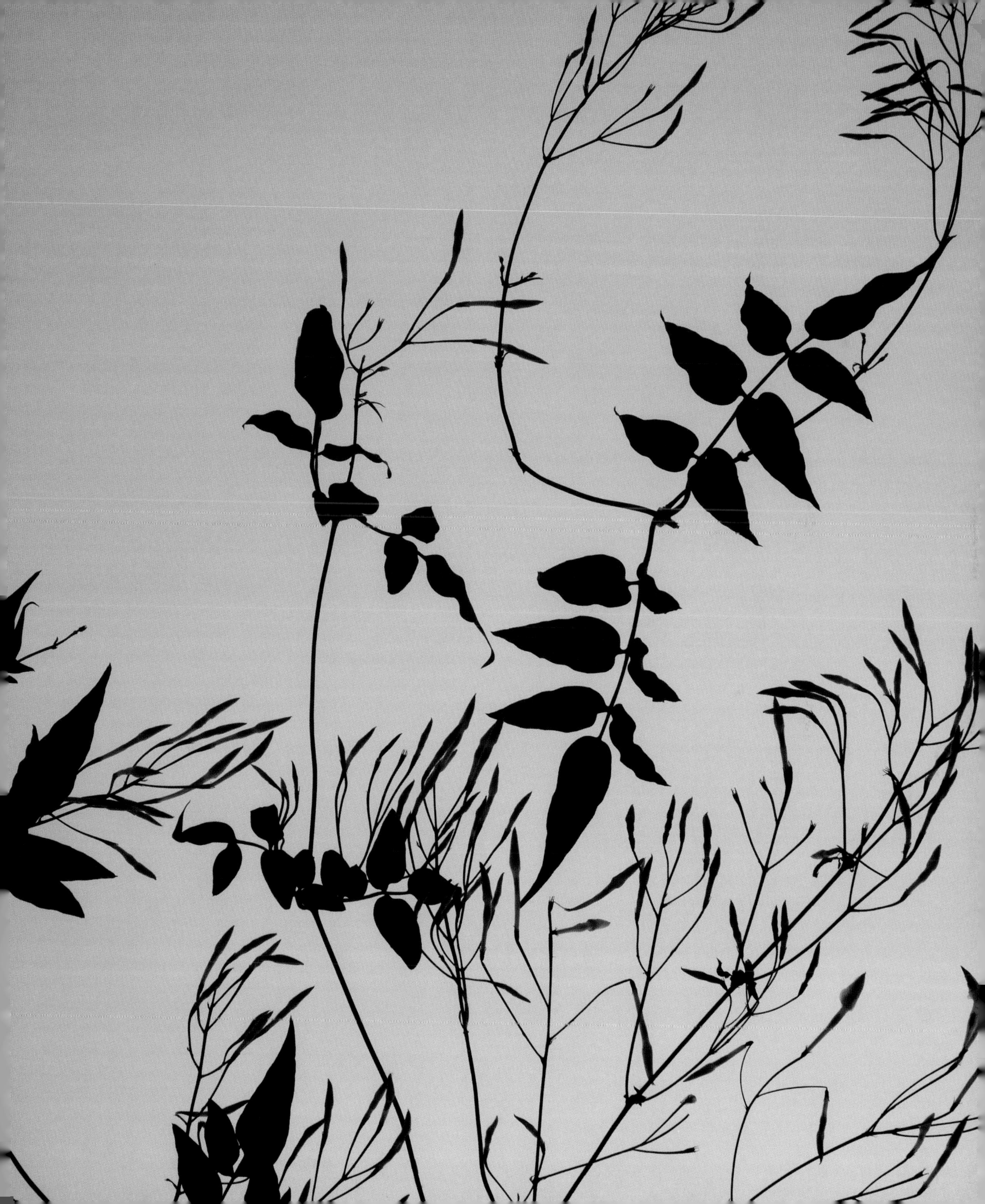

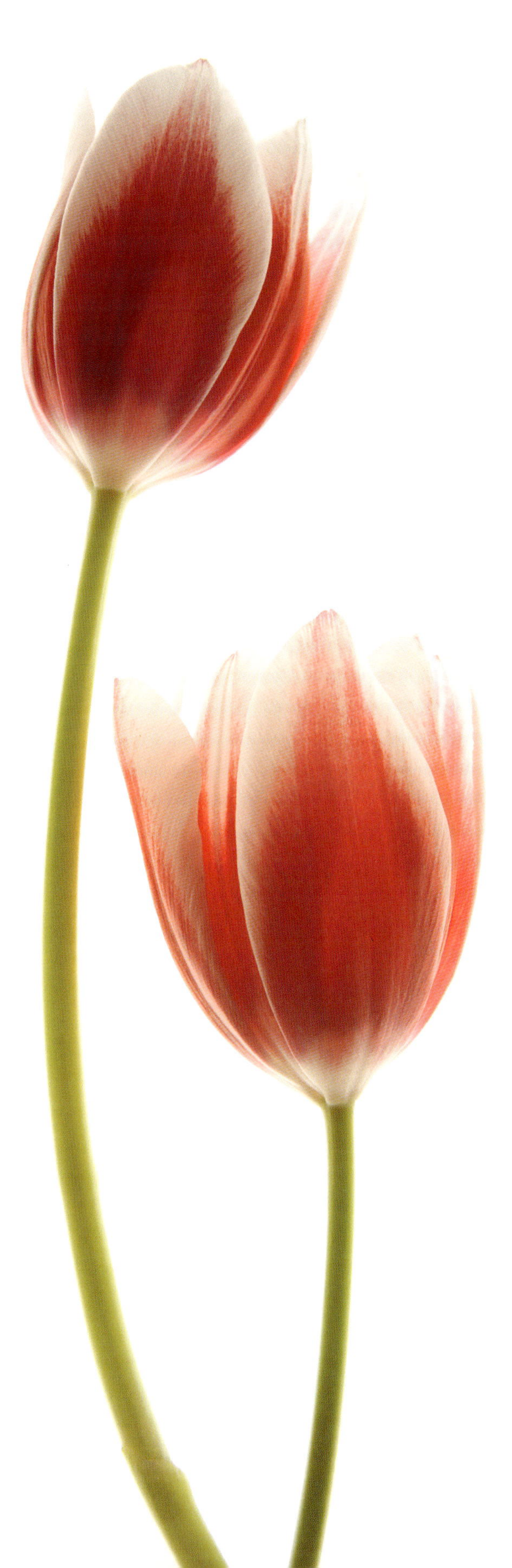

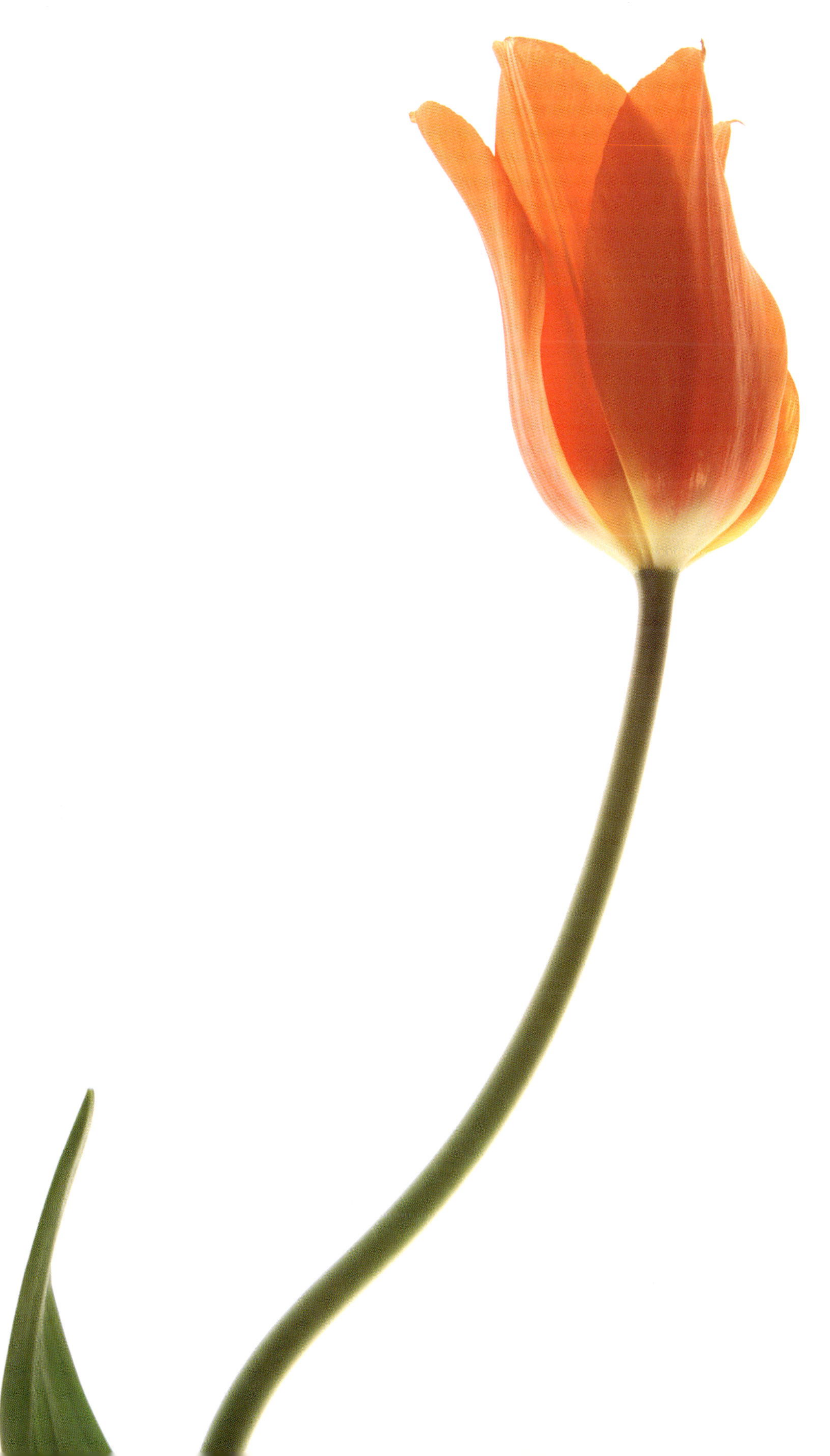

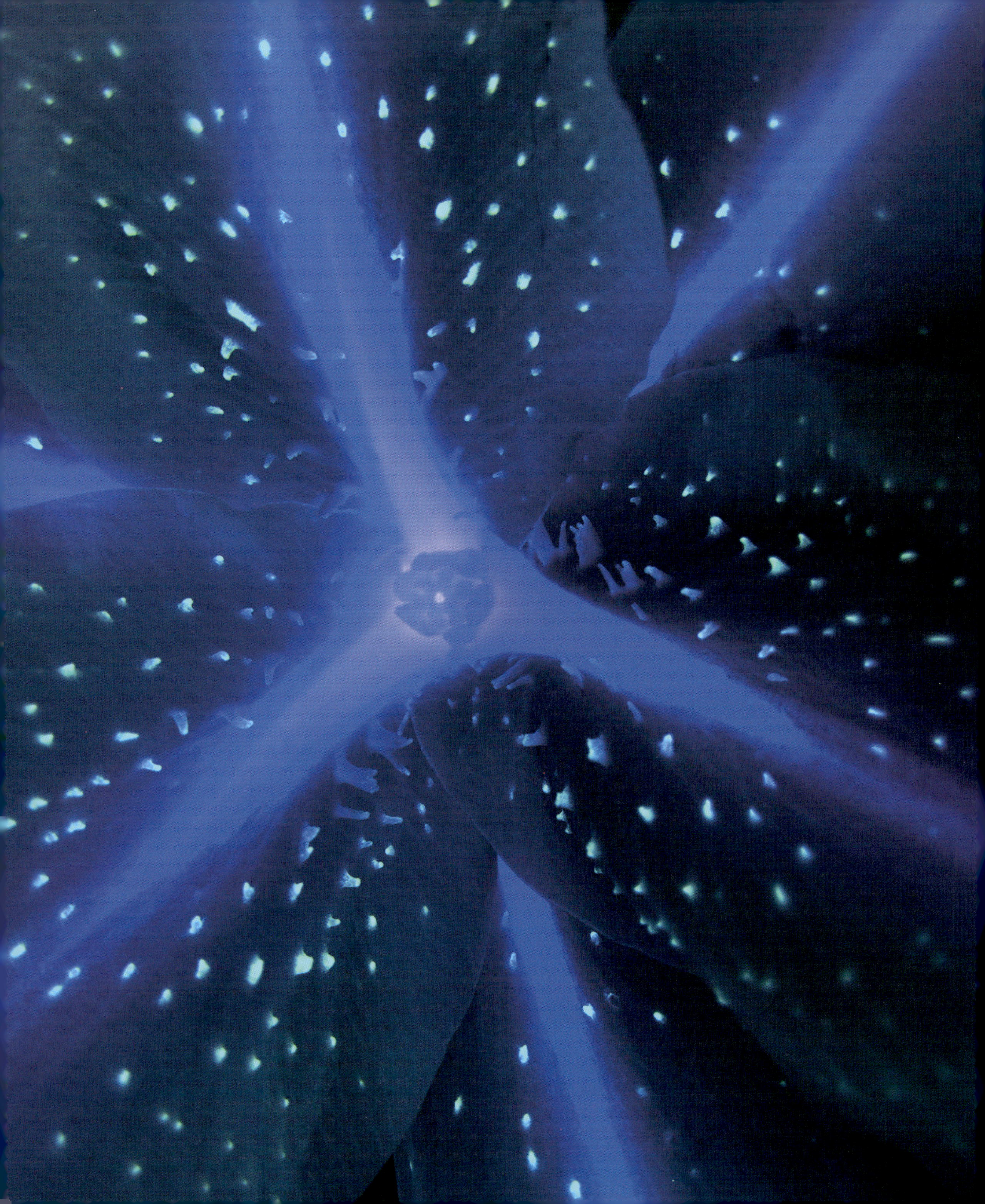

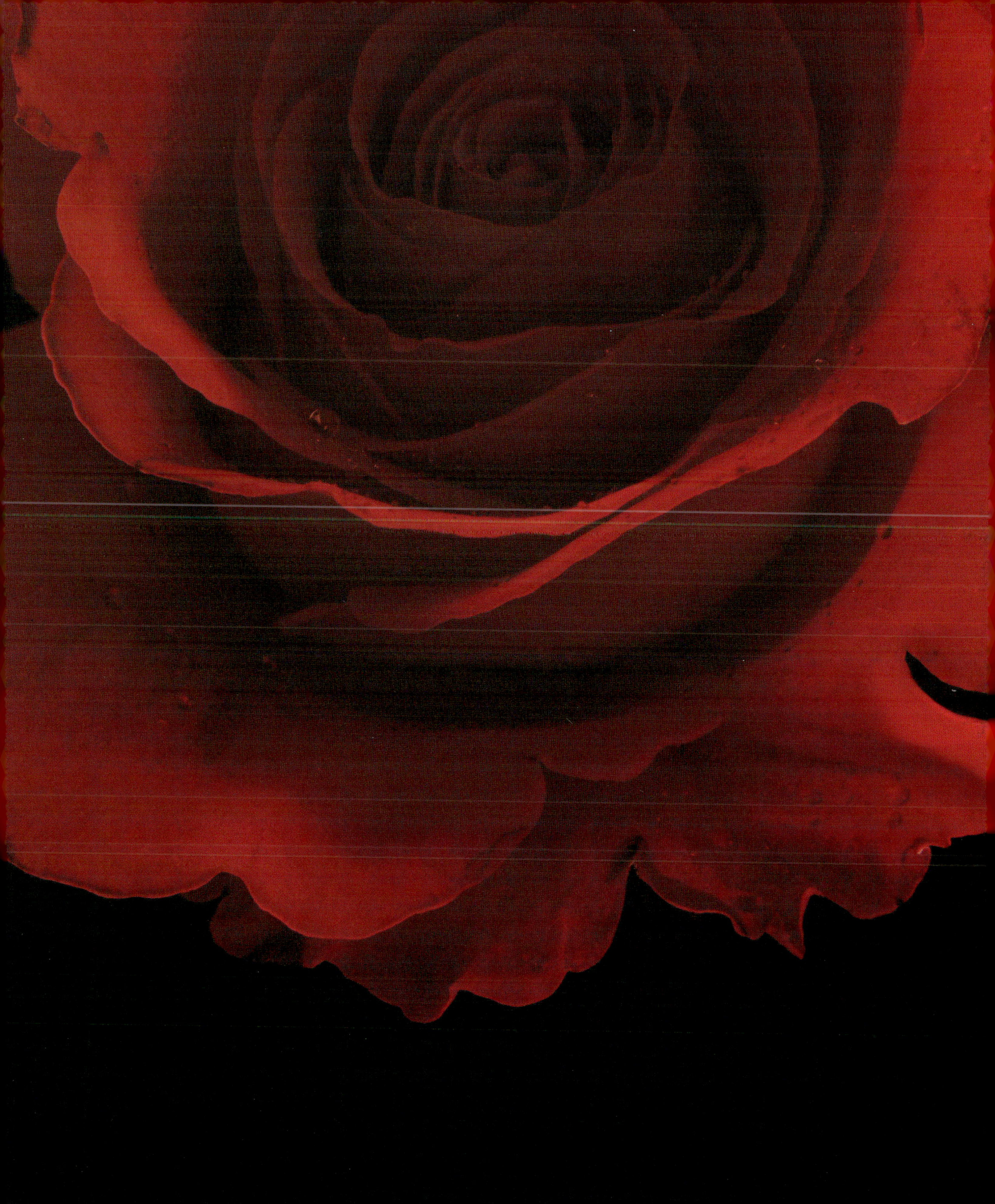

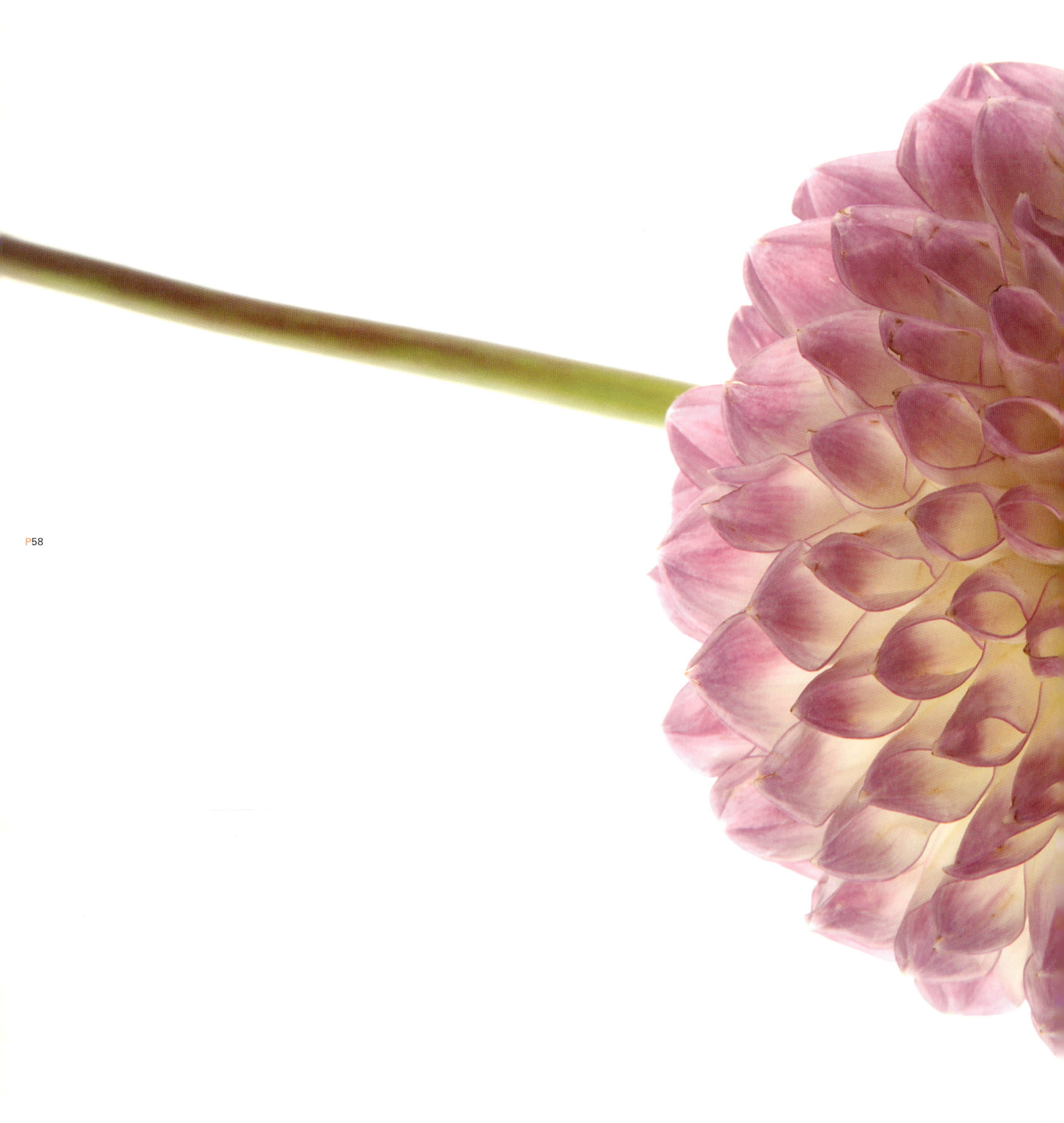

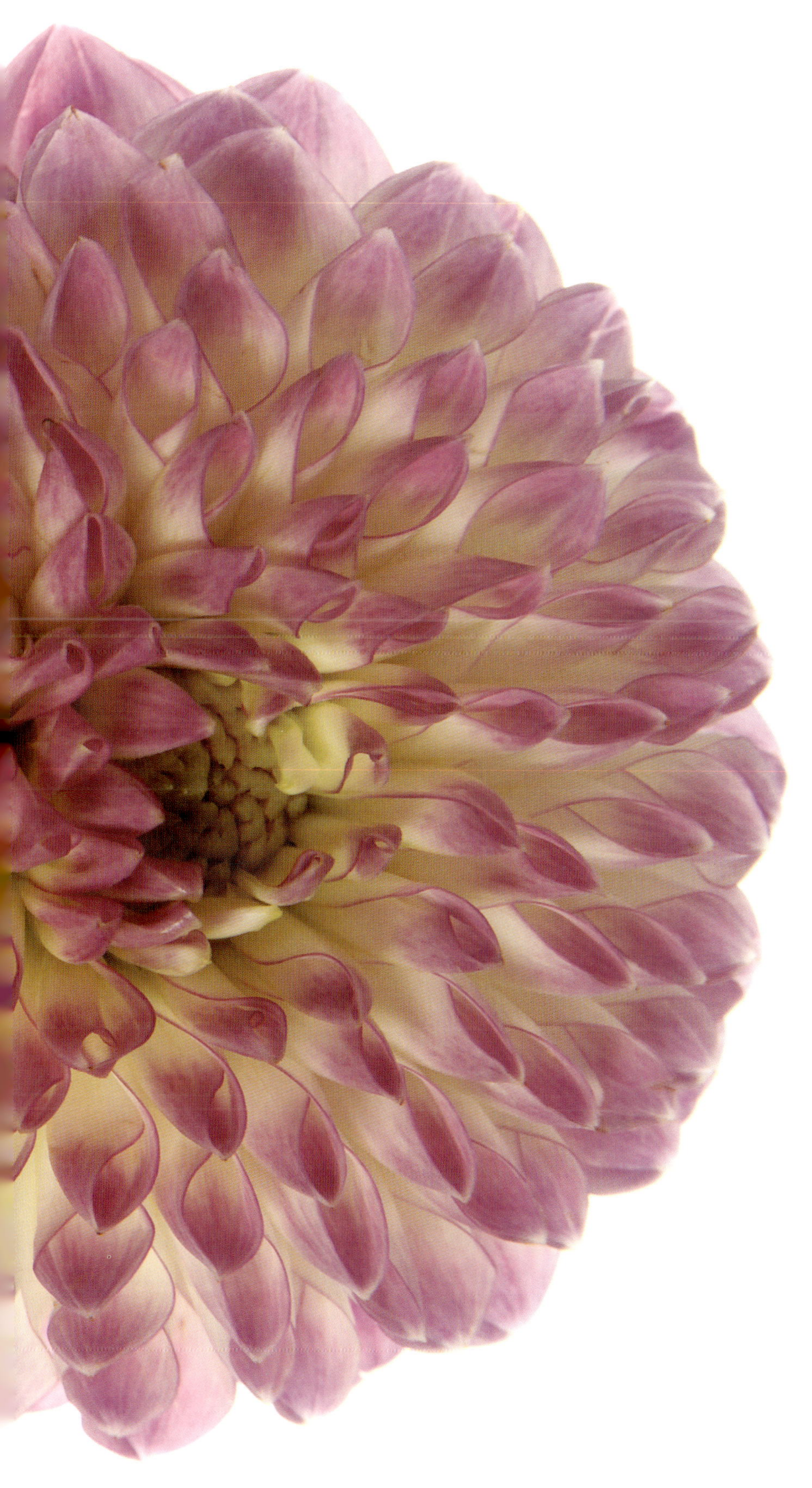

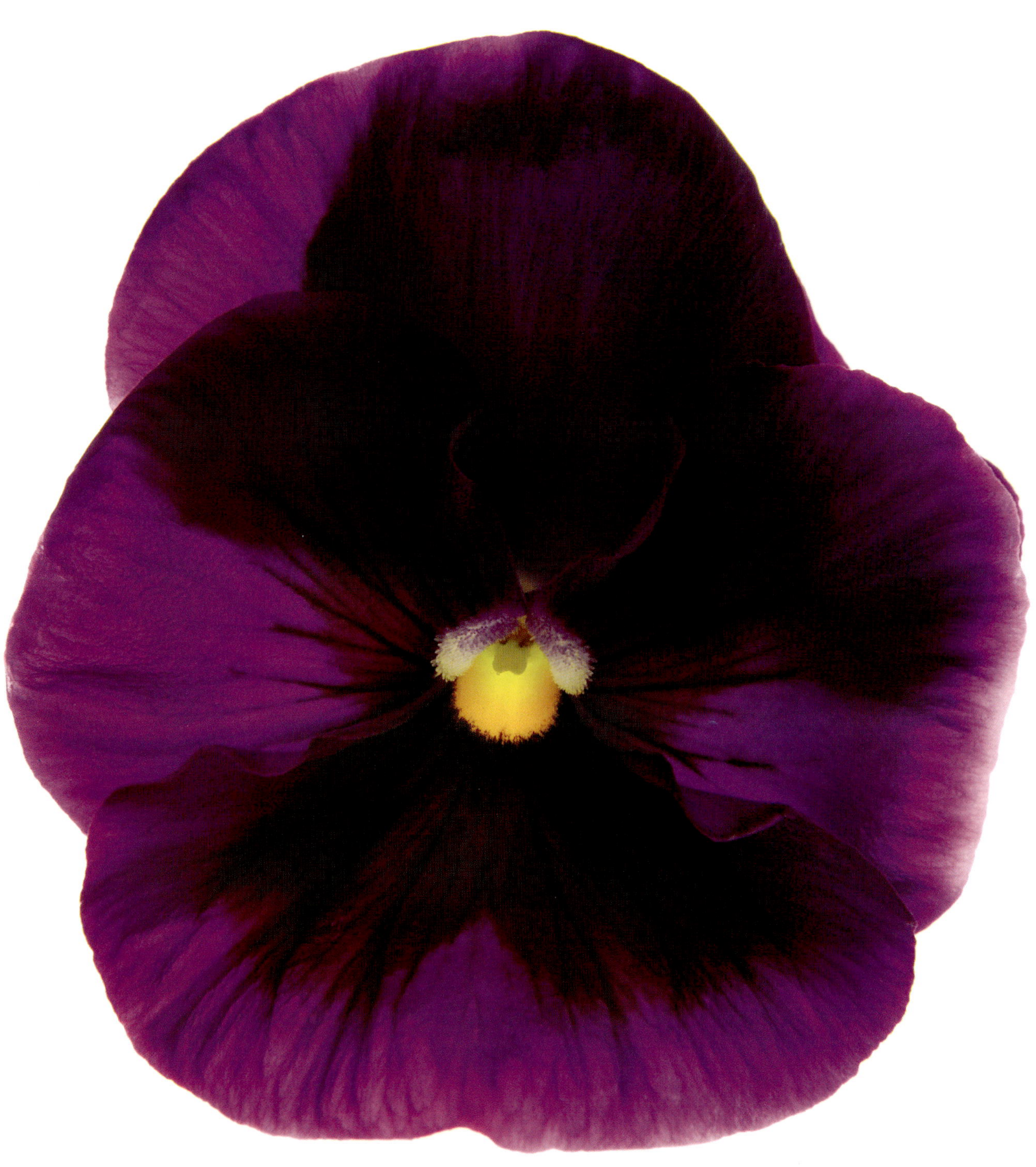

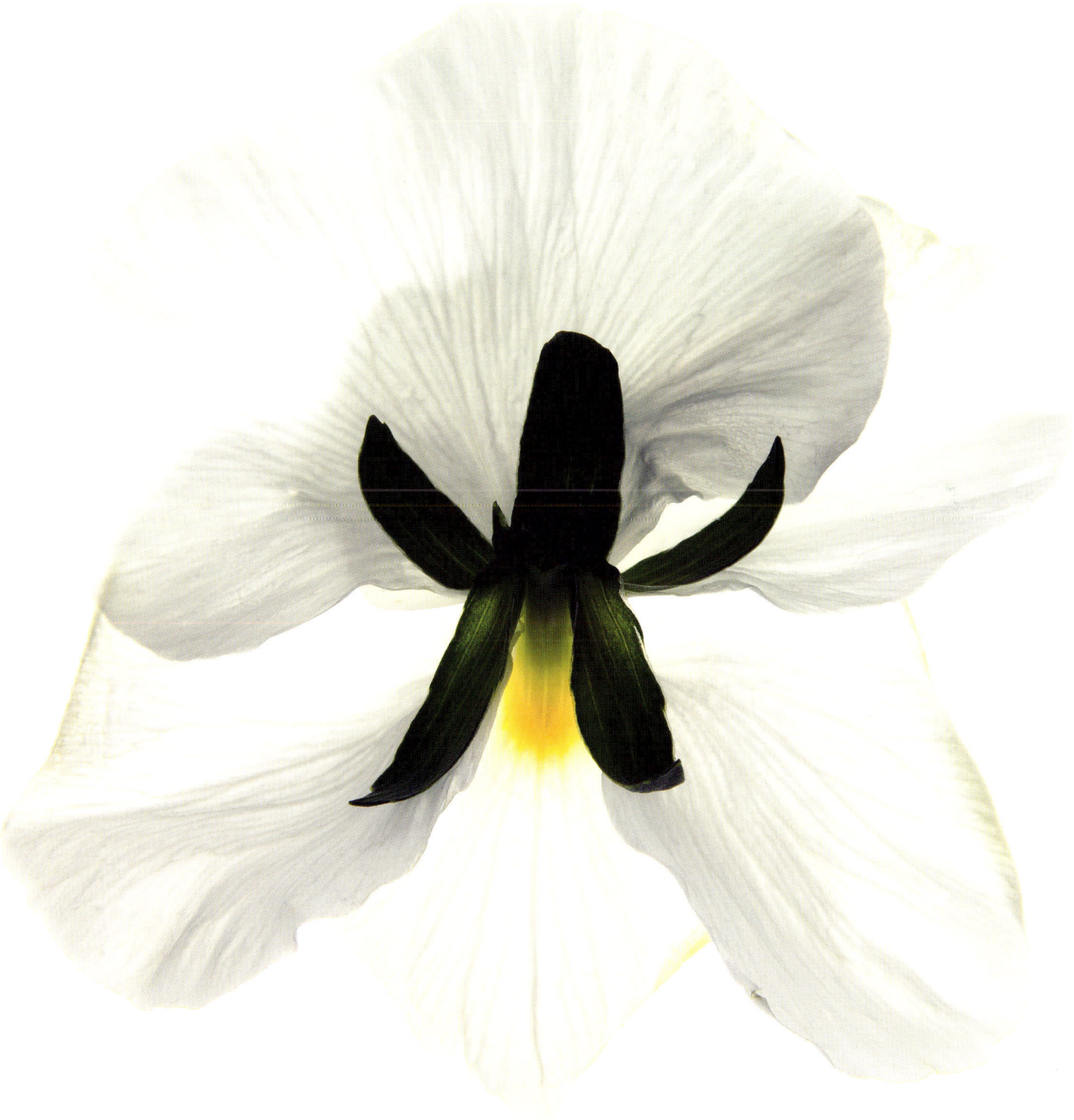

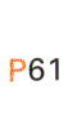

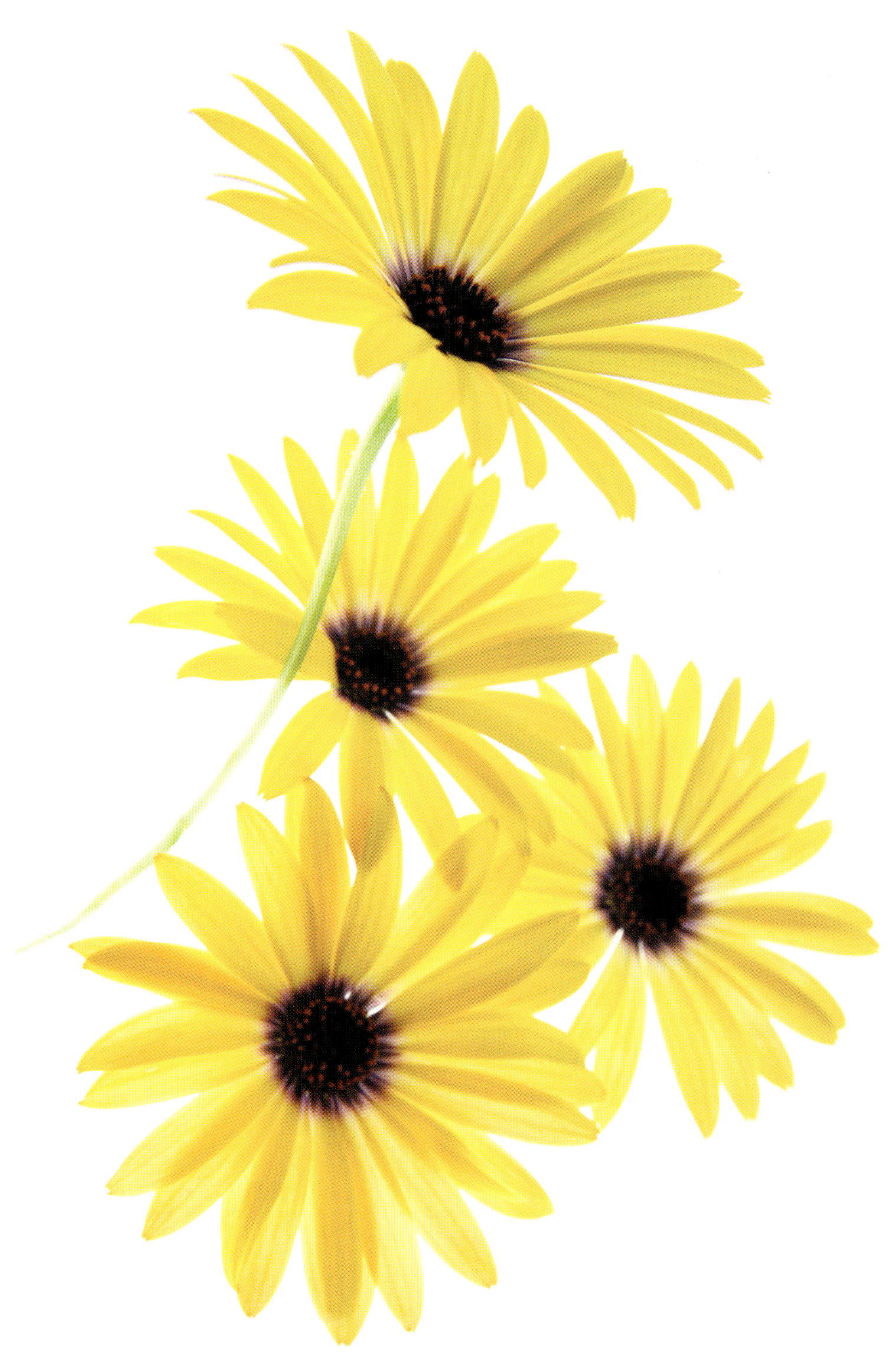

P62

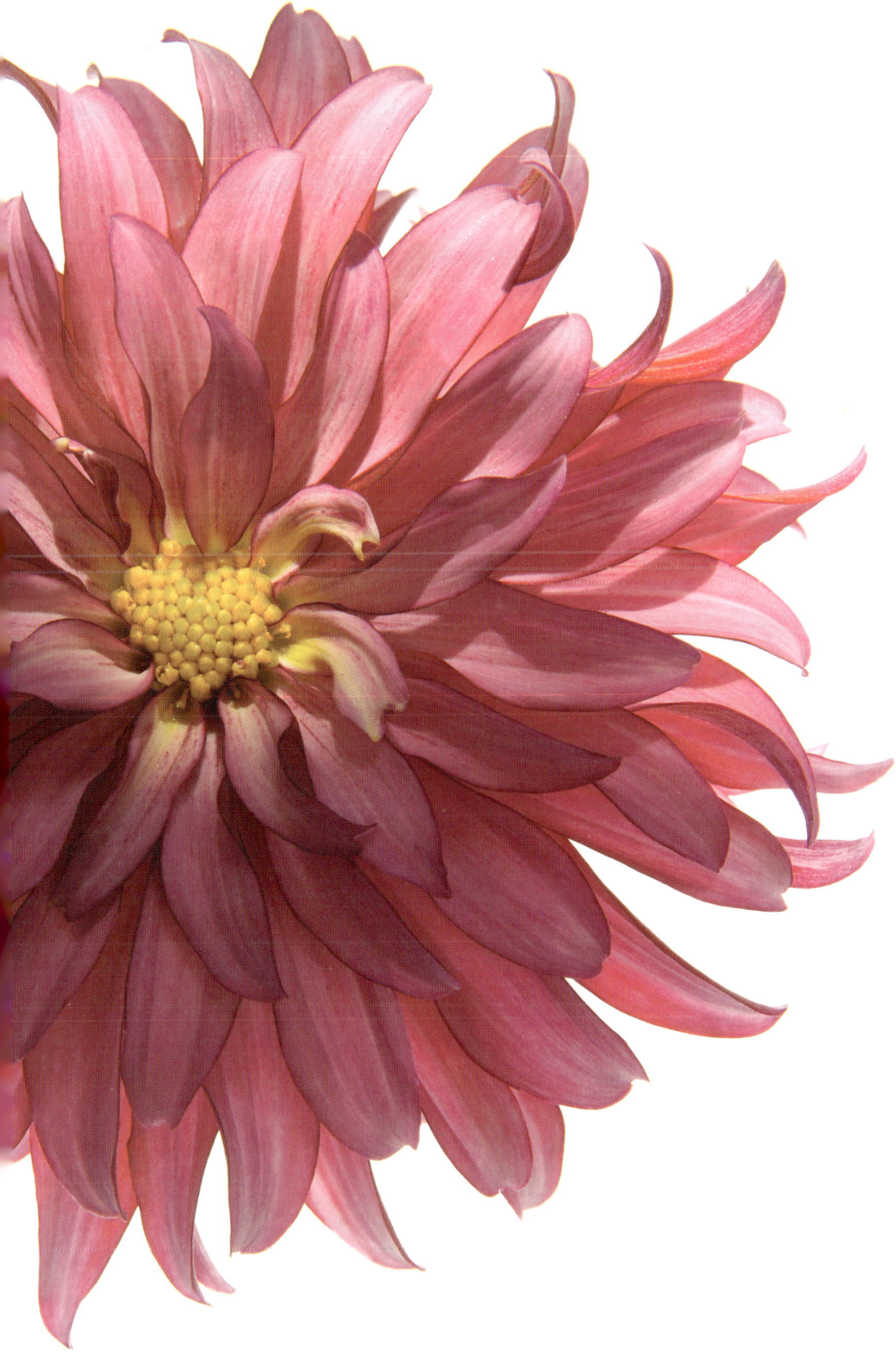

P63

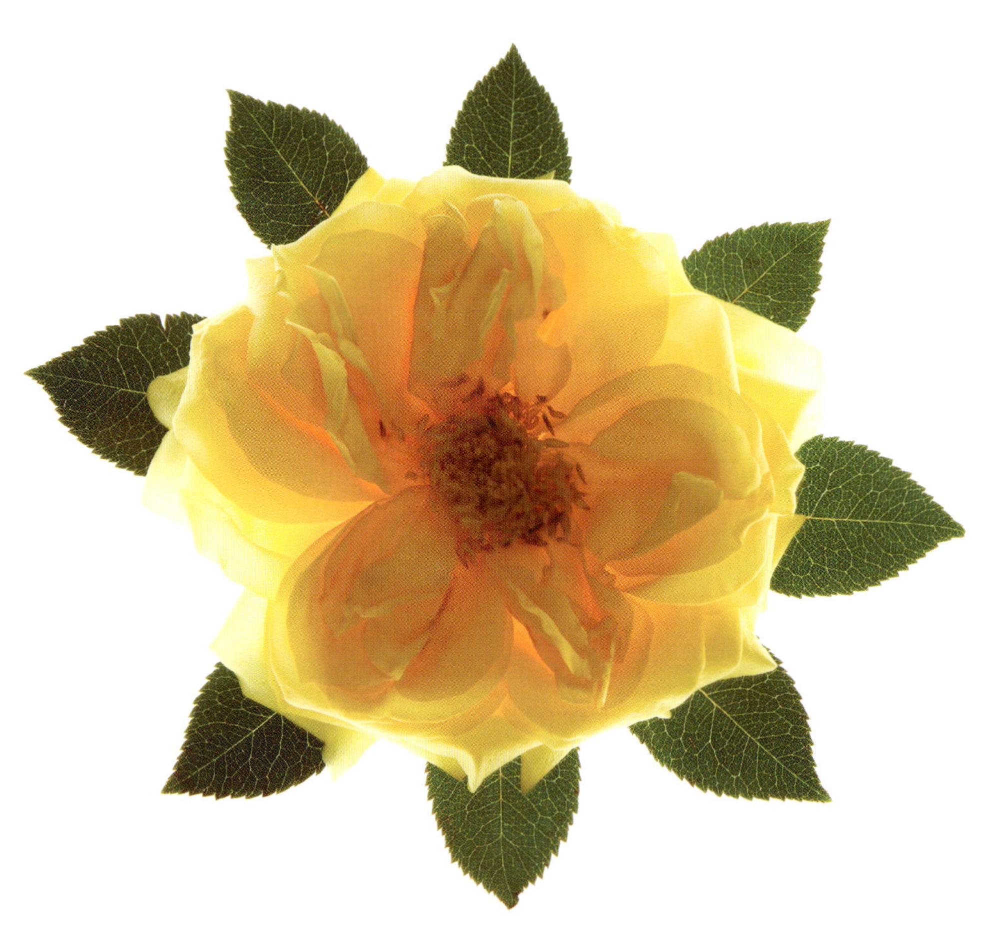

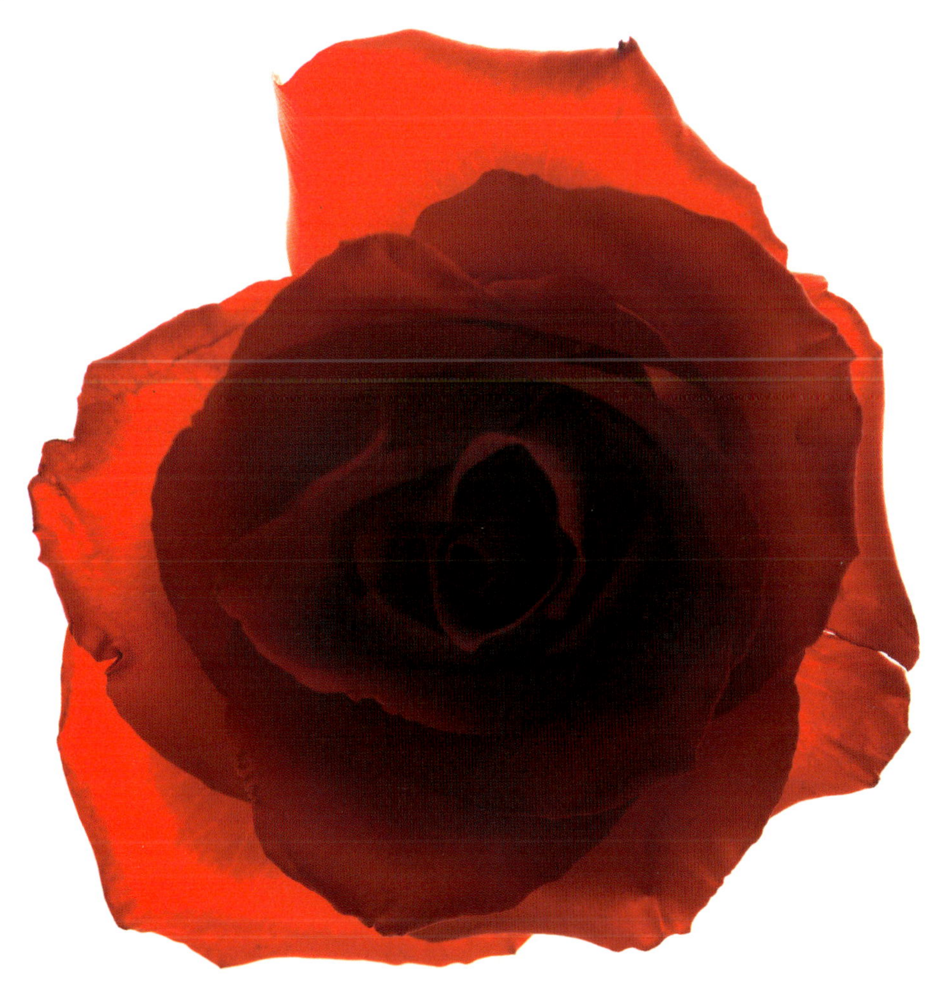

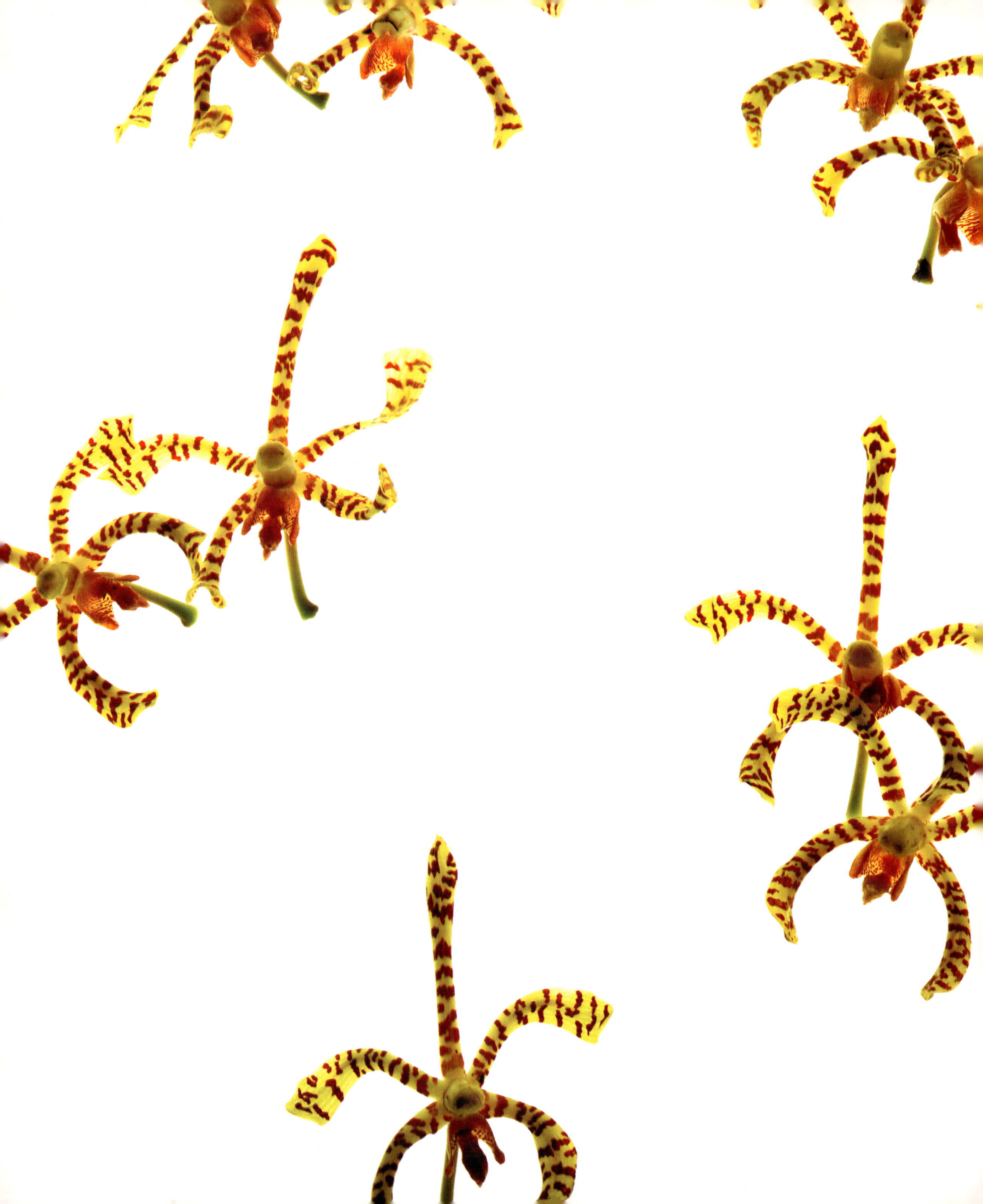

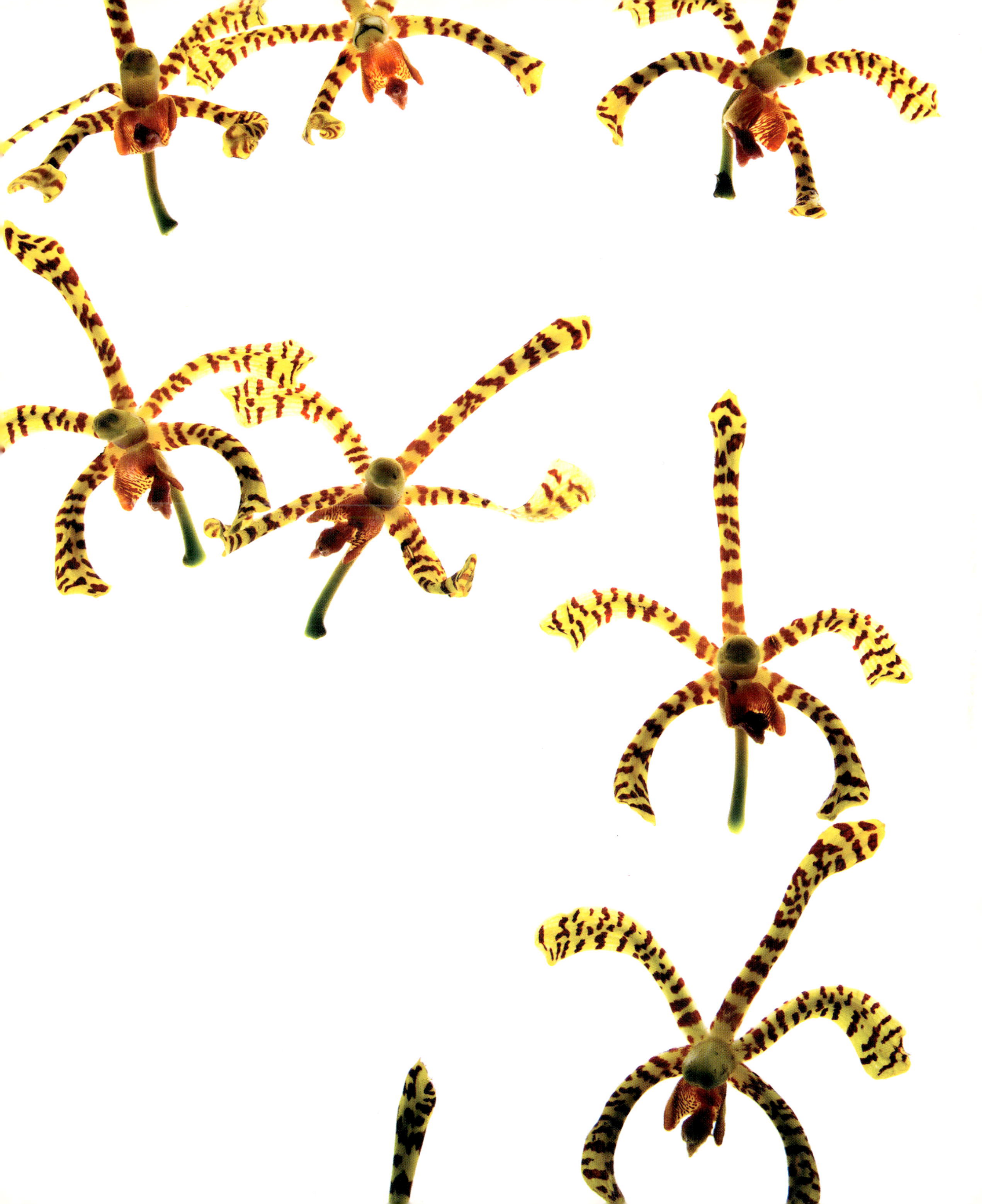

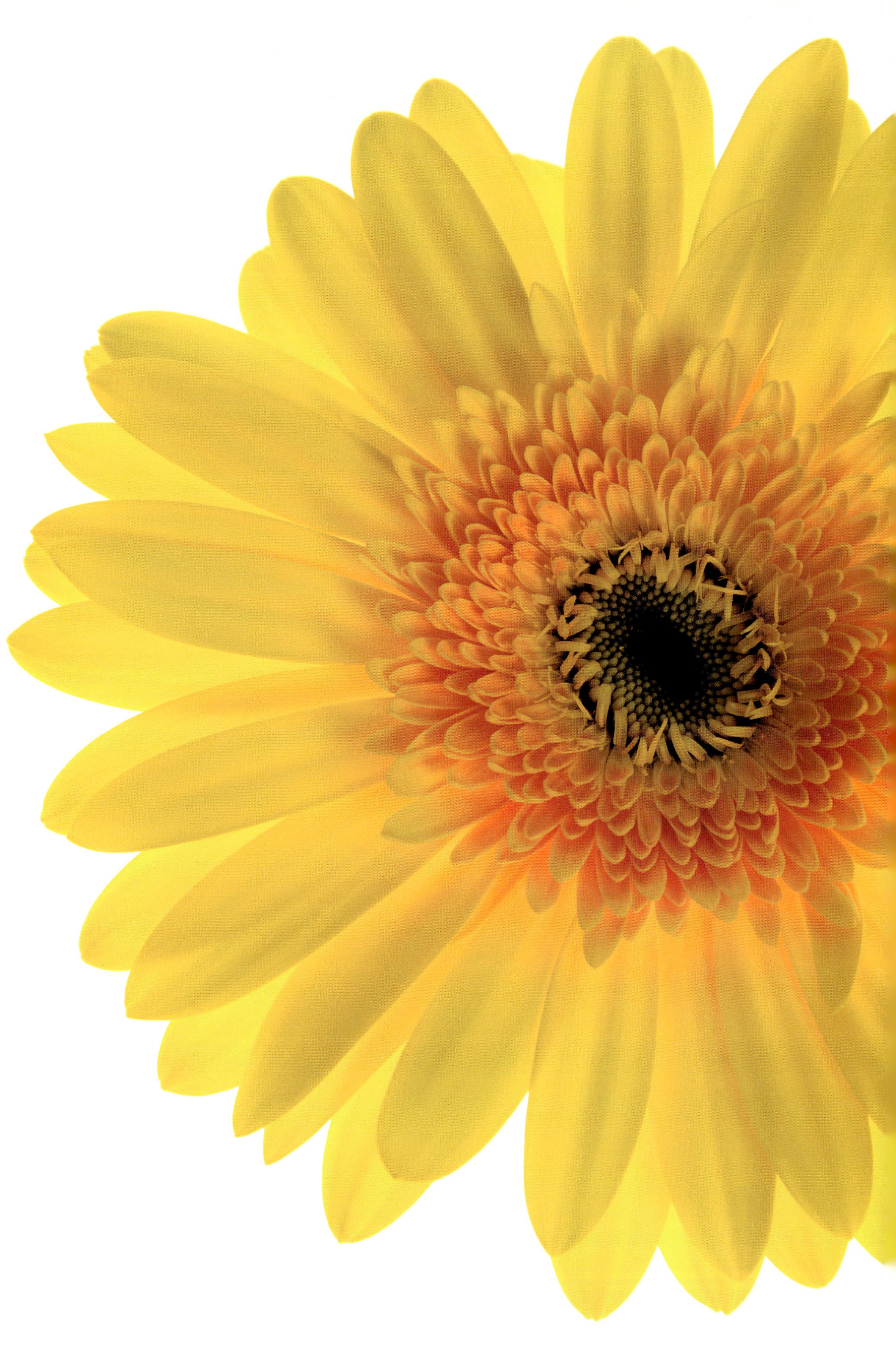

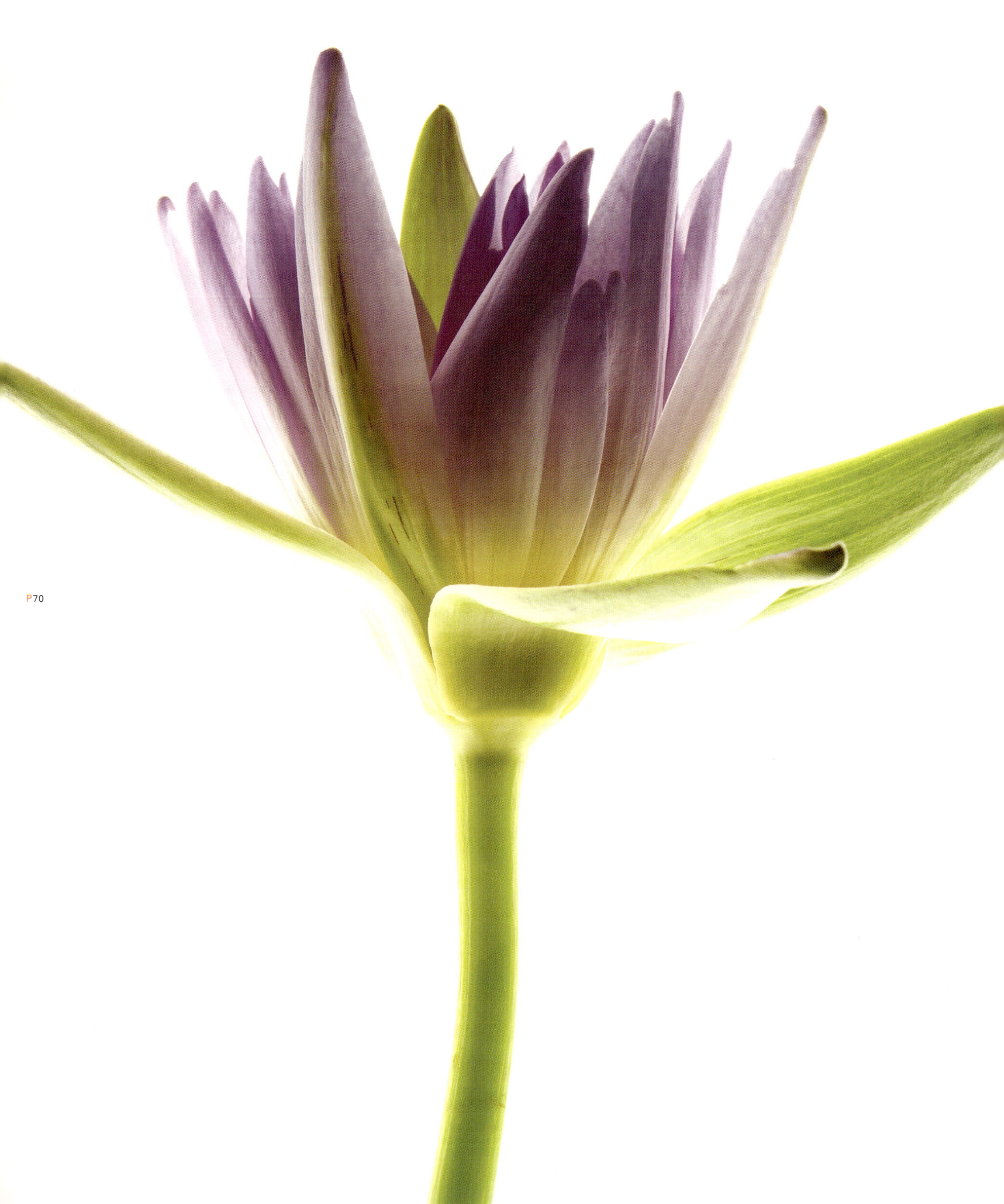

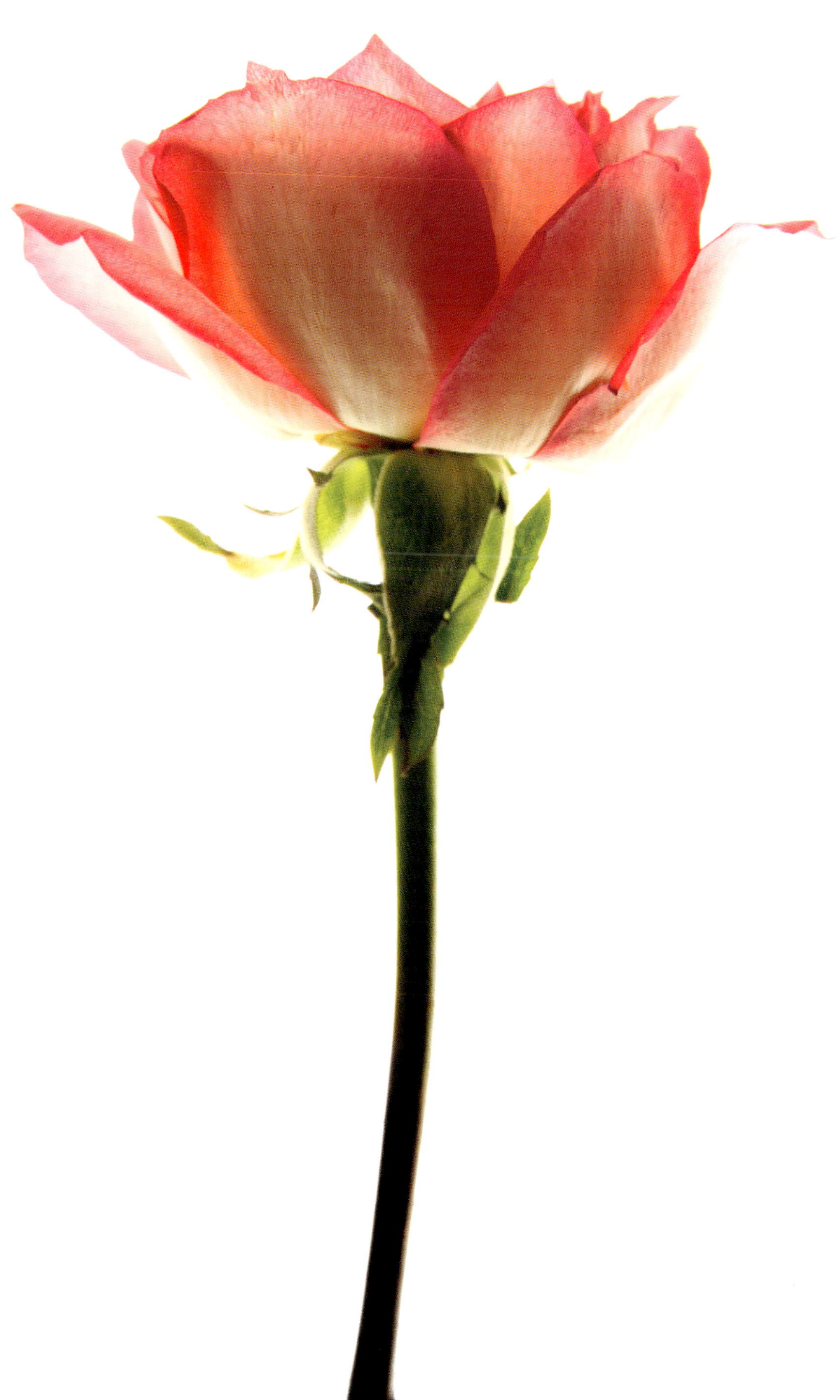

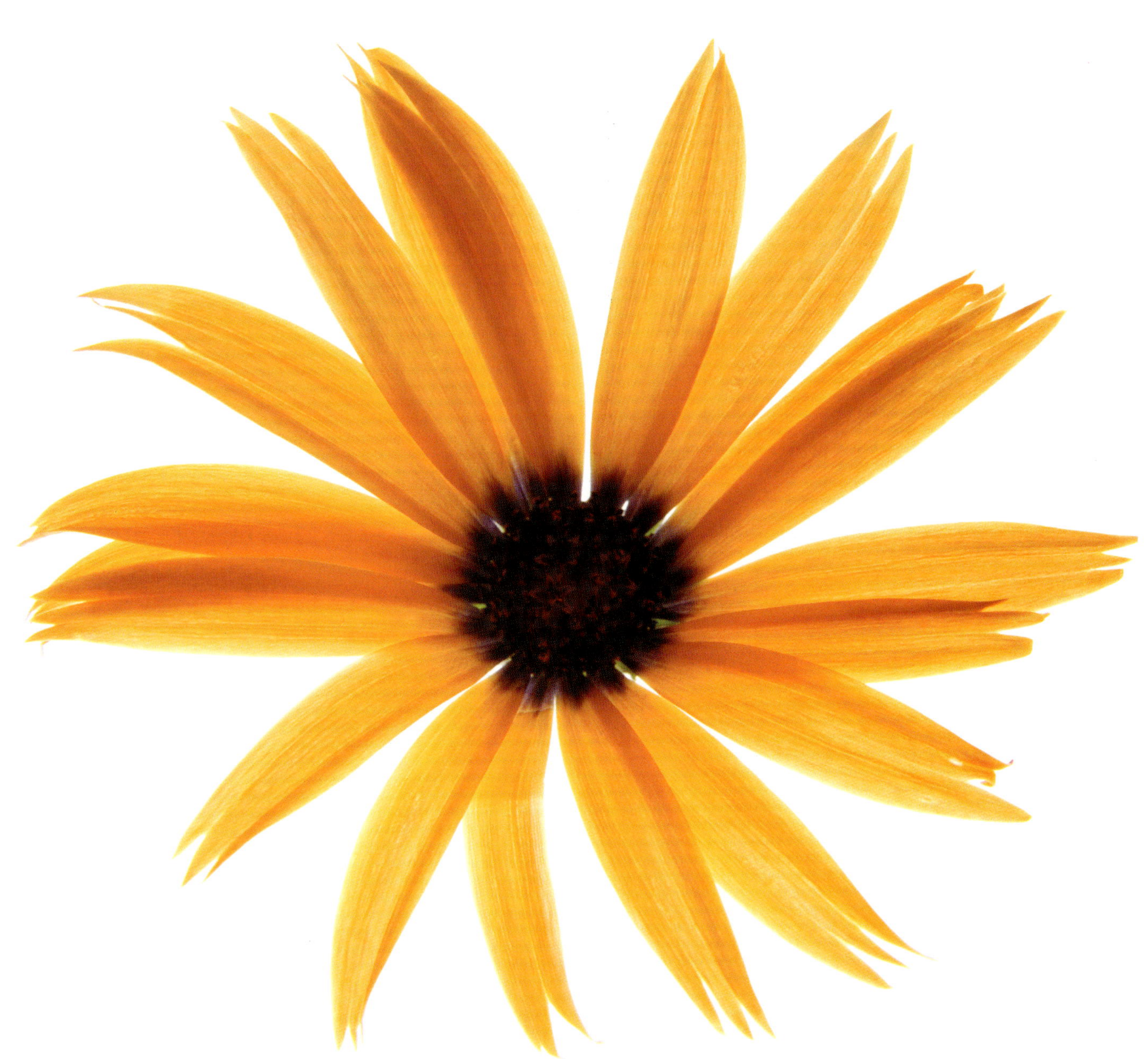

P72

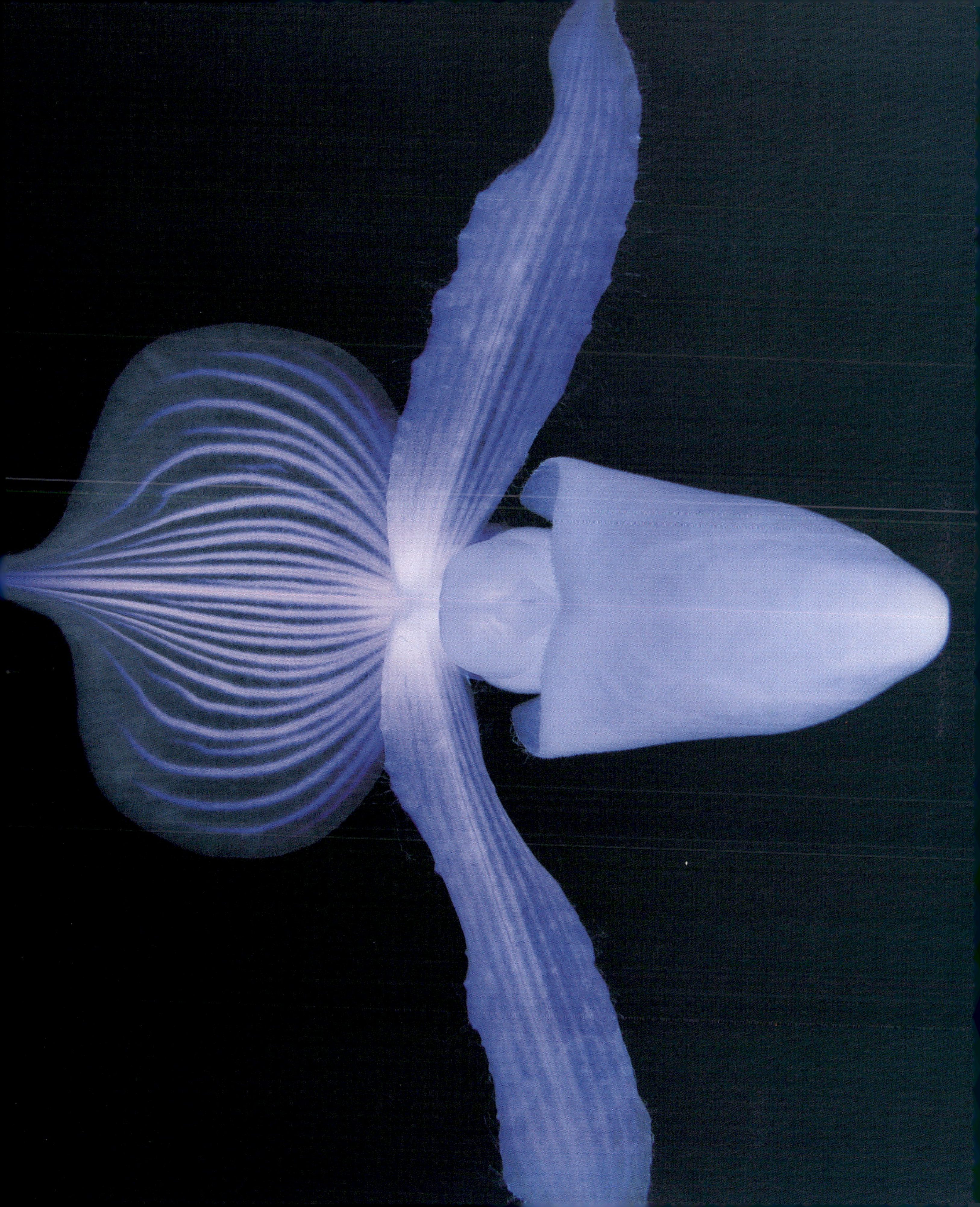

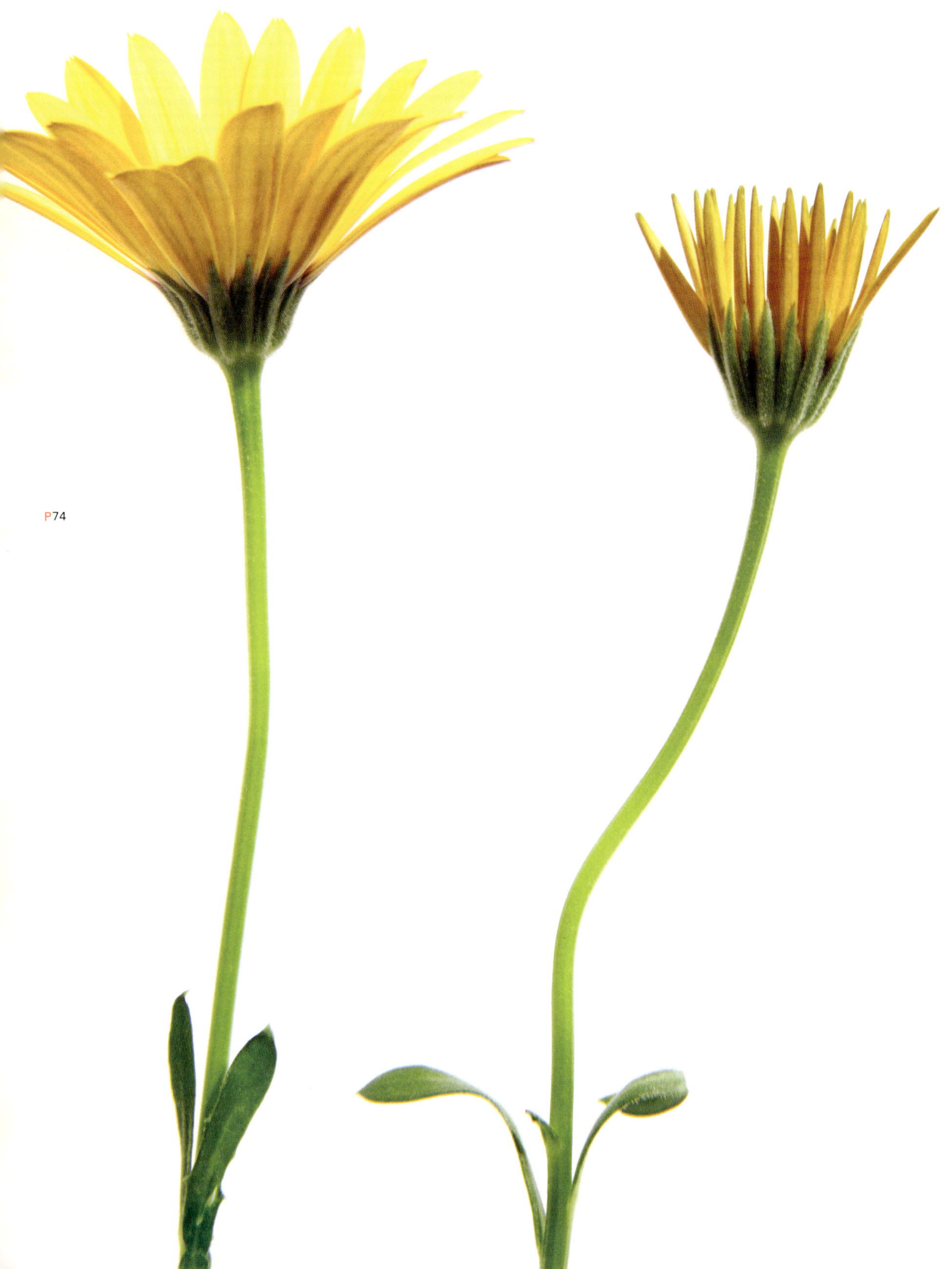

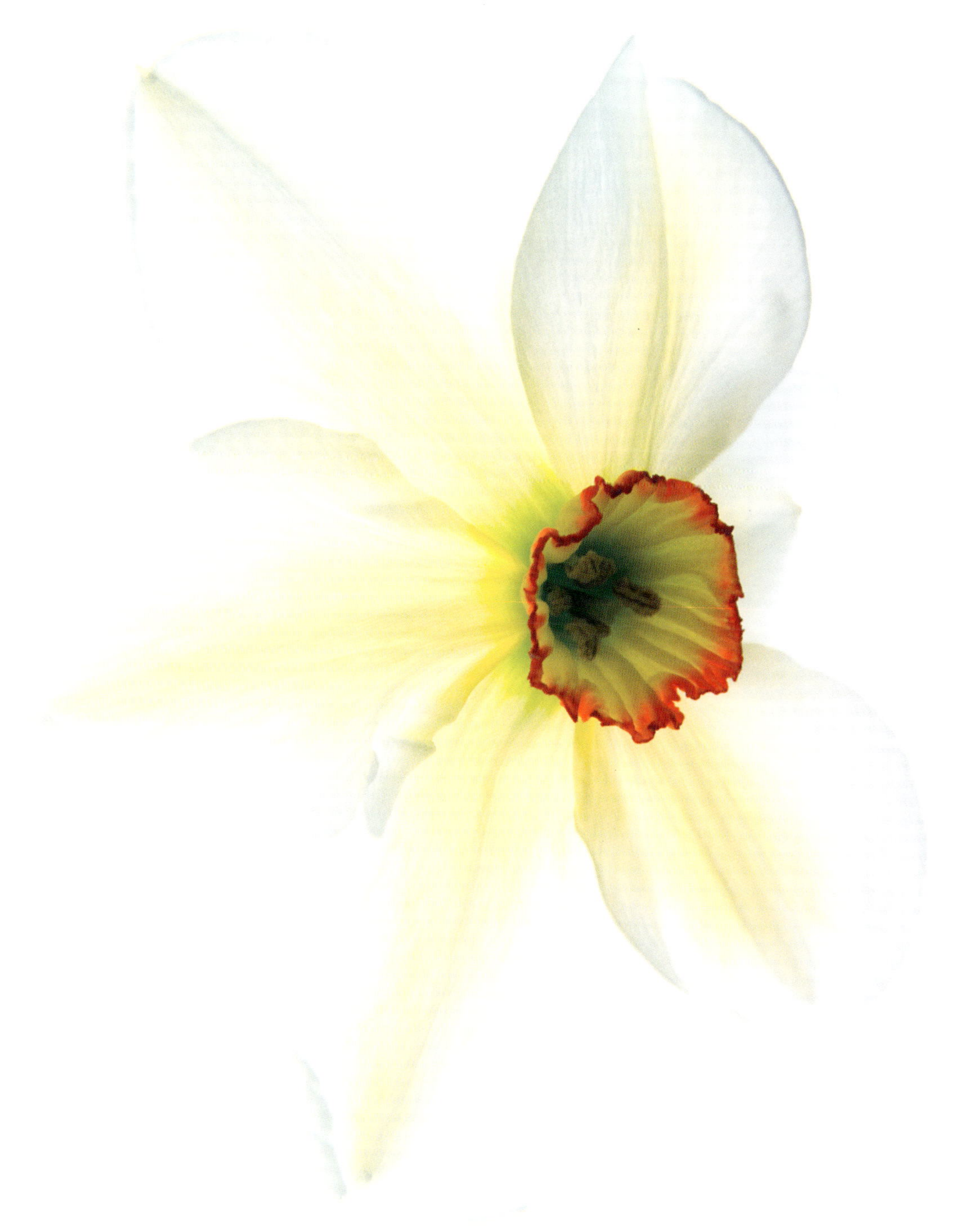

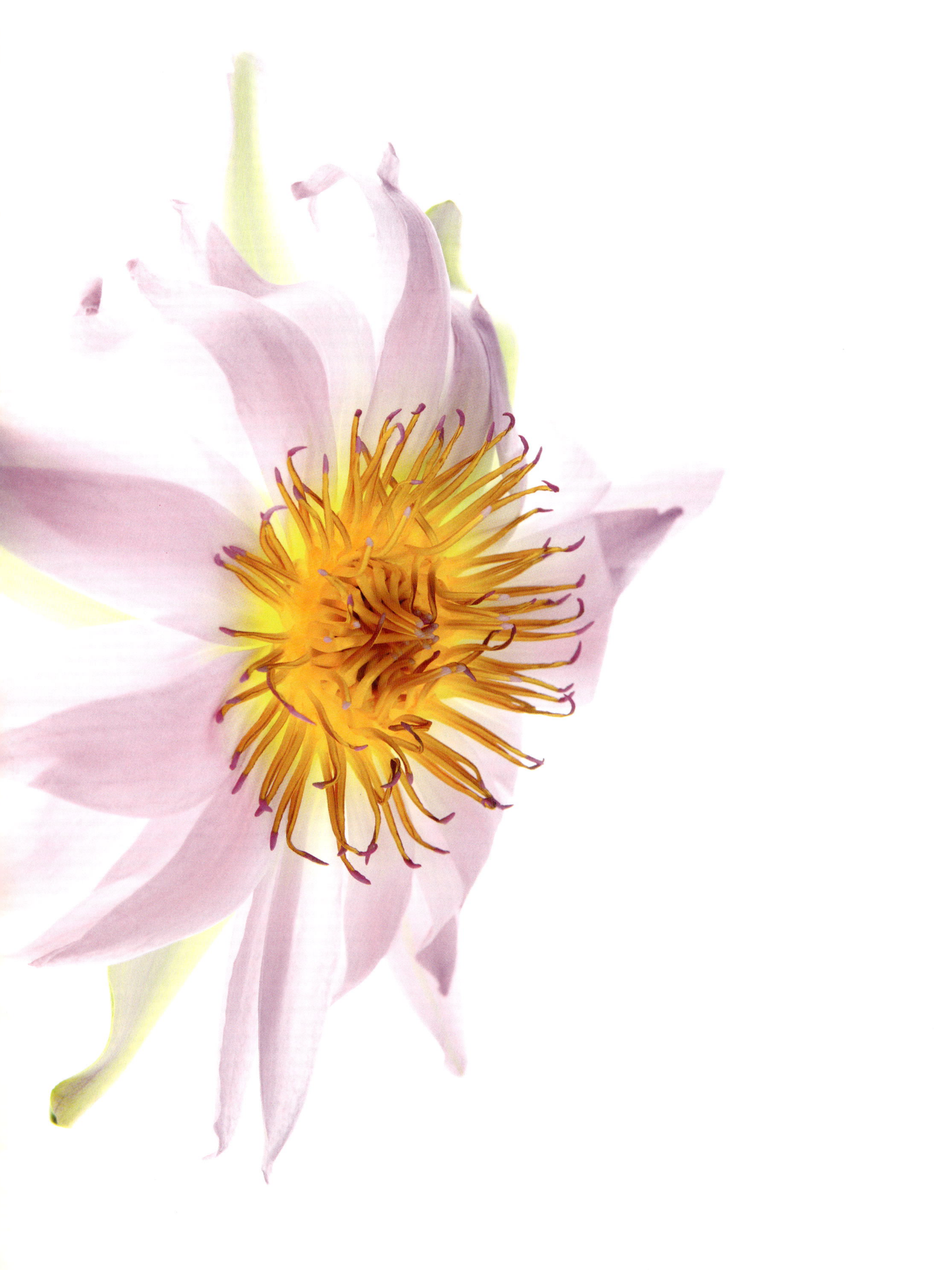

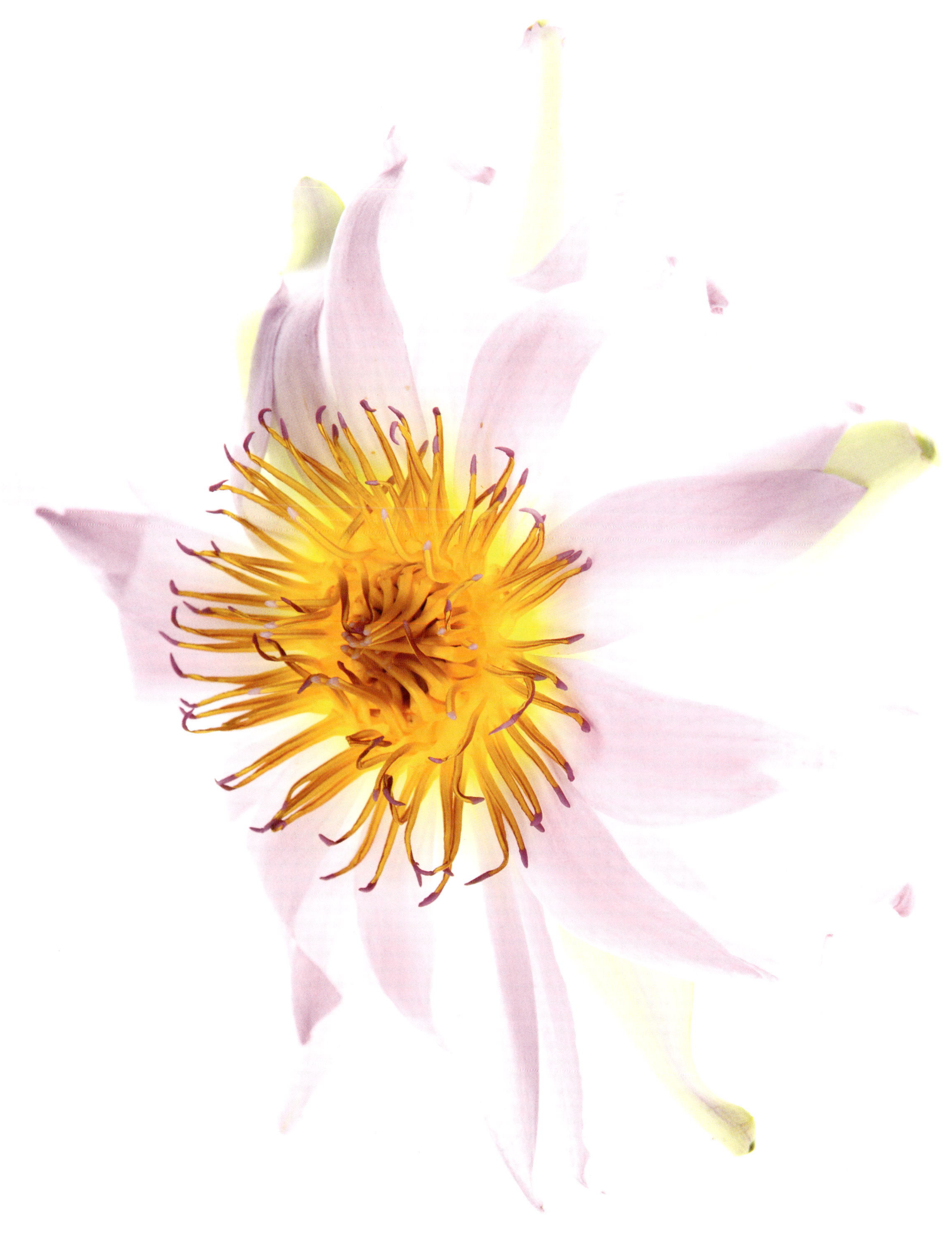

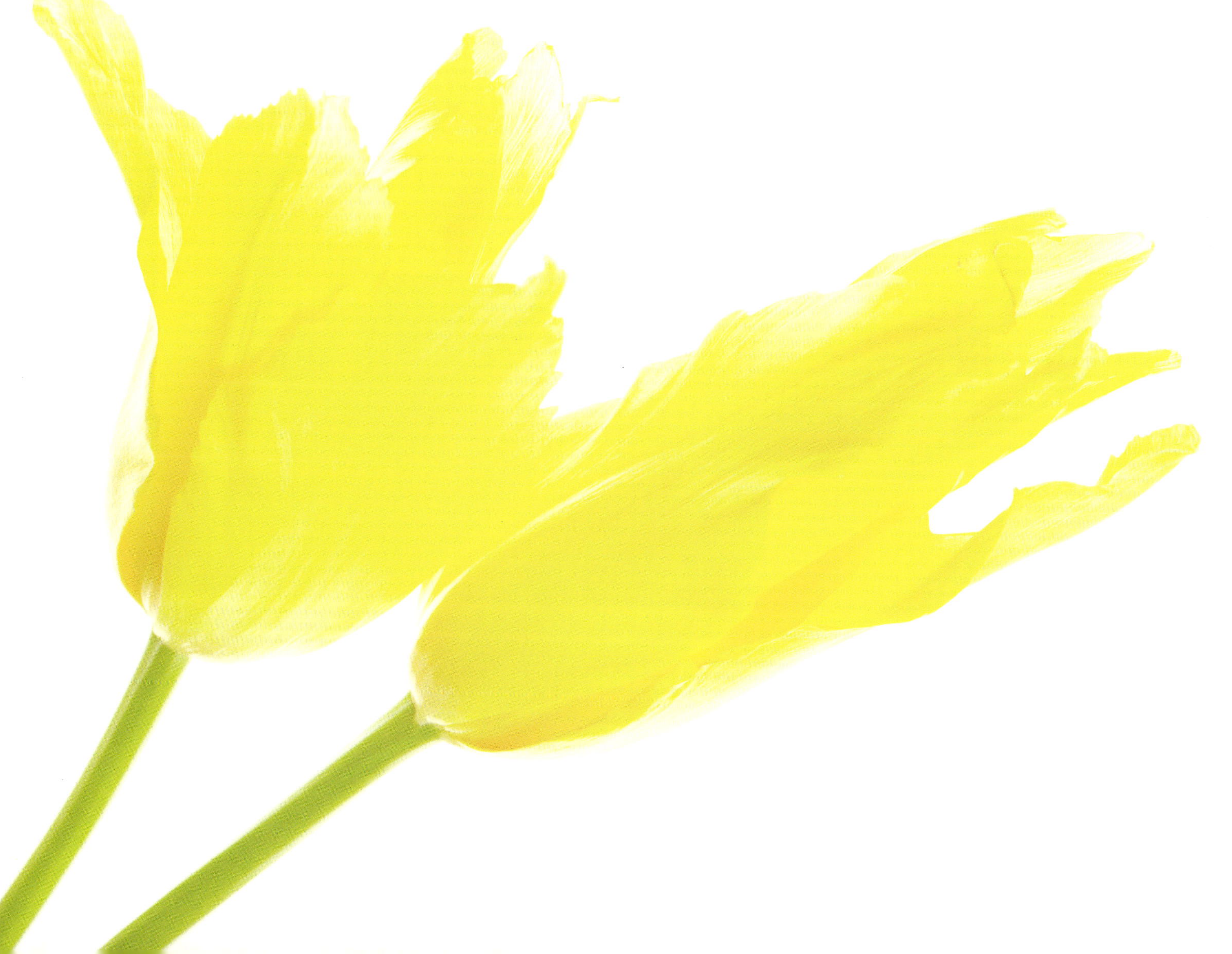

p 80

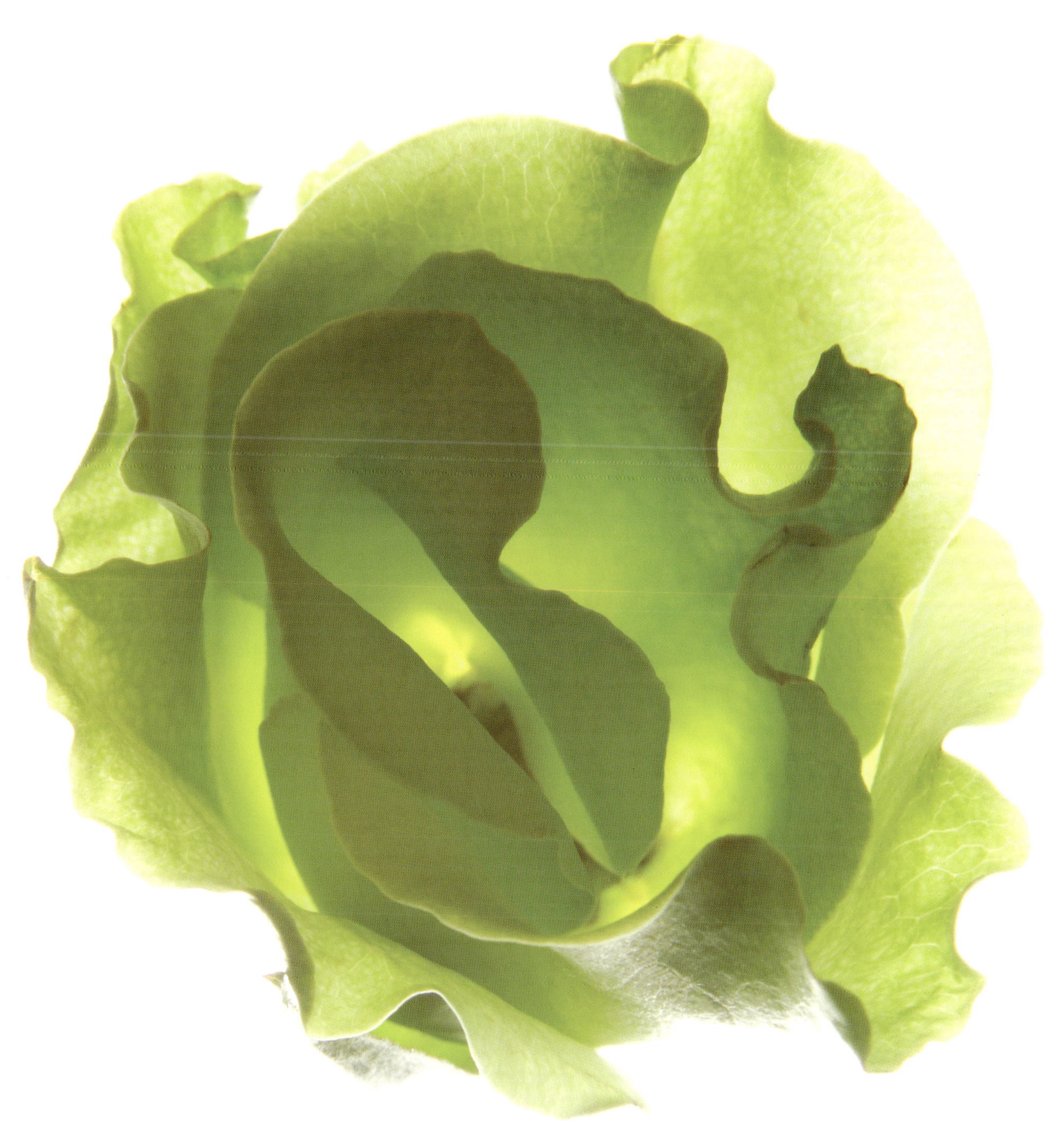

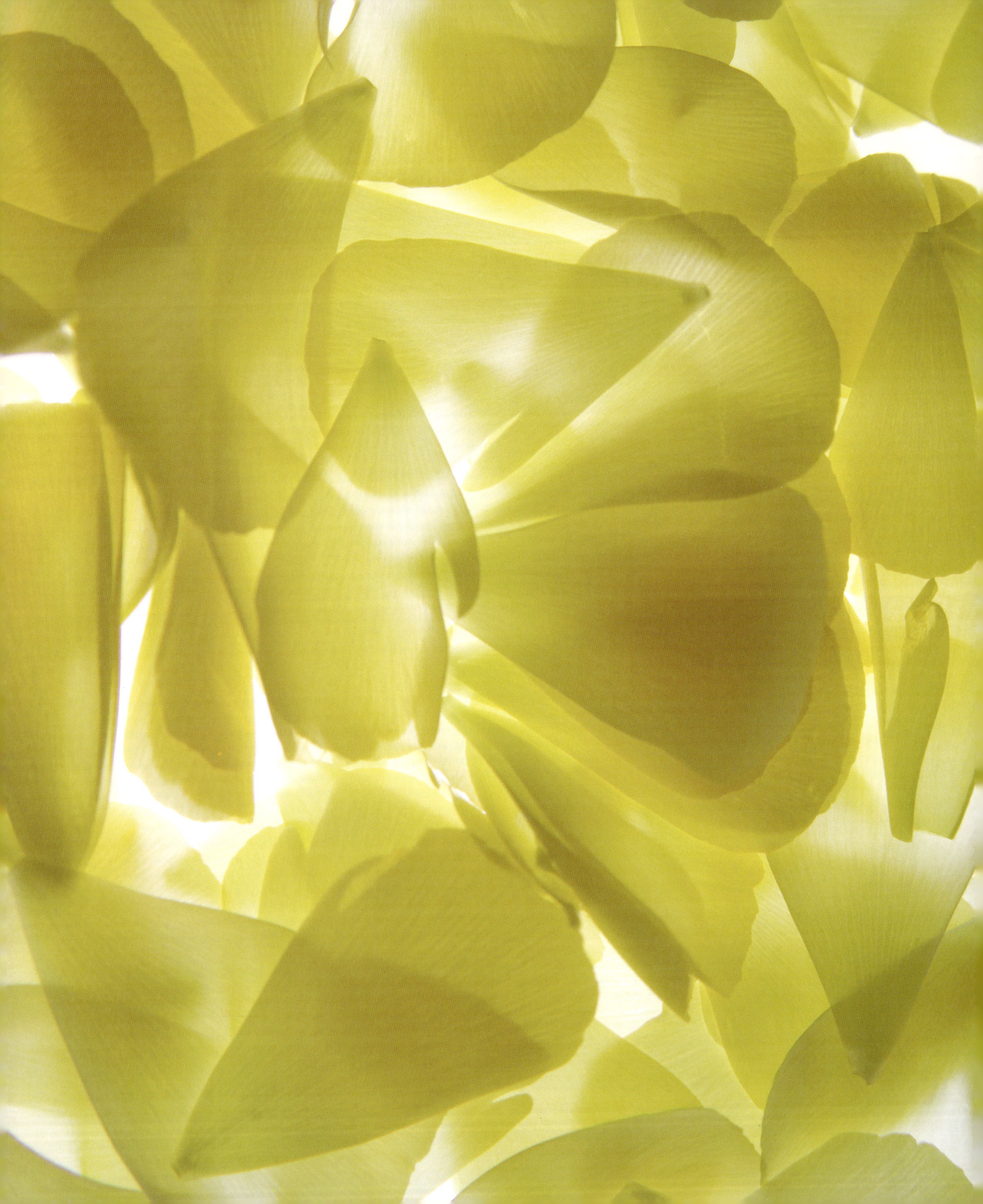

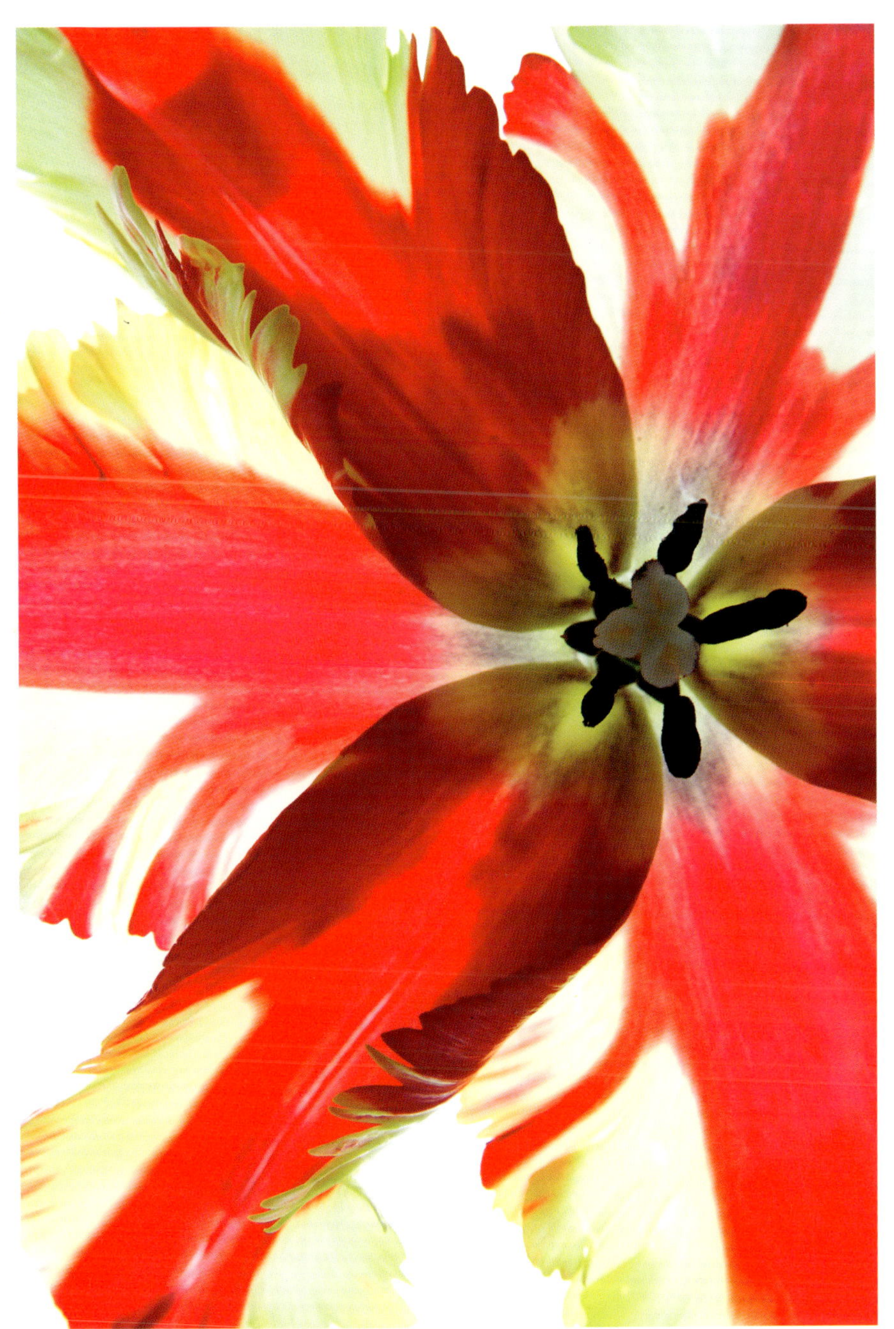

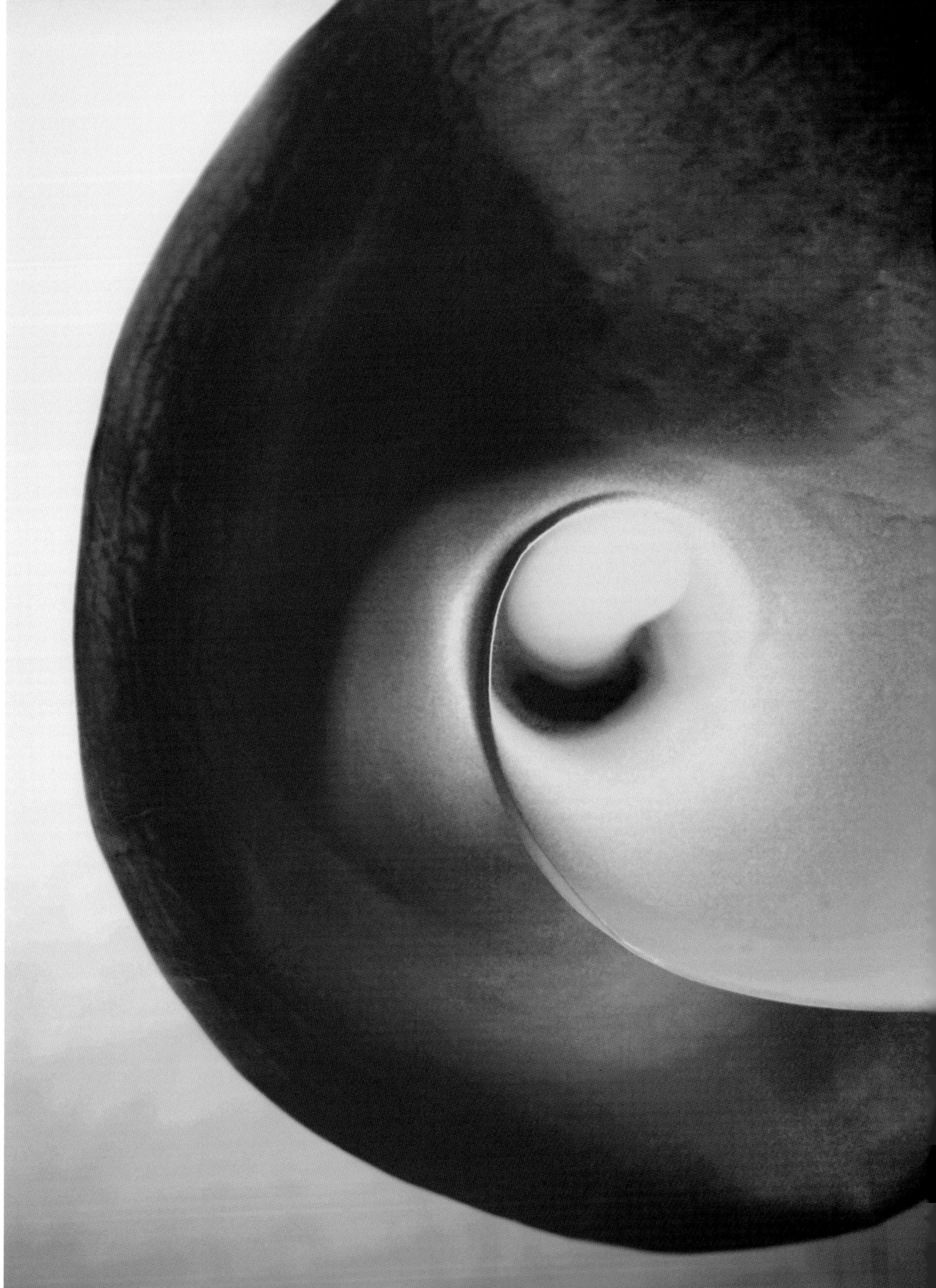

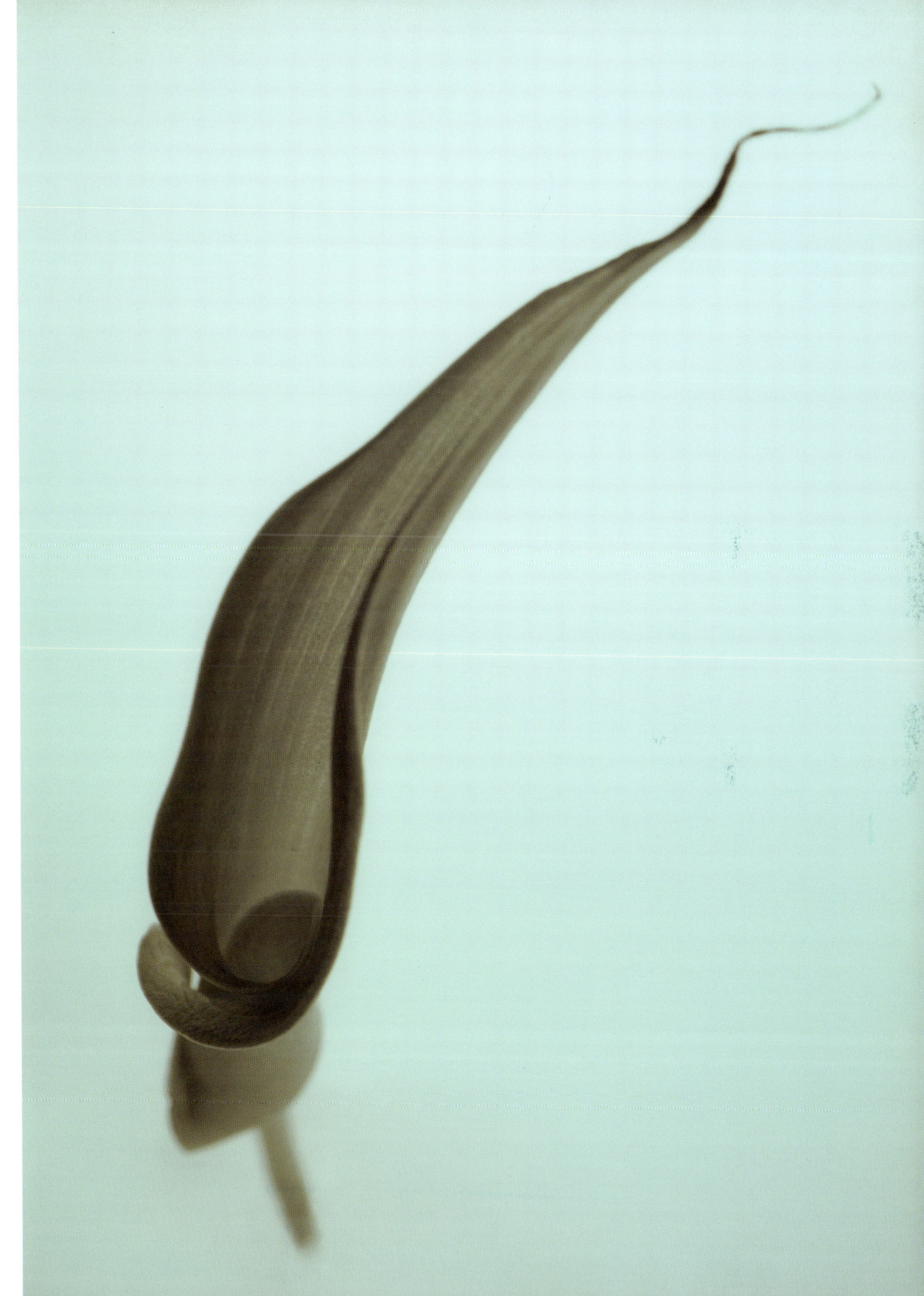

P86

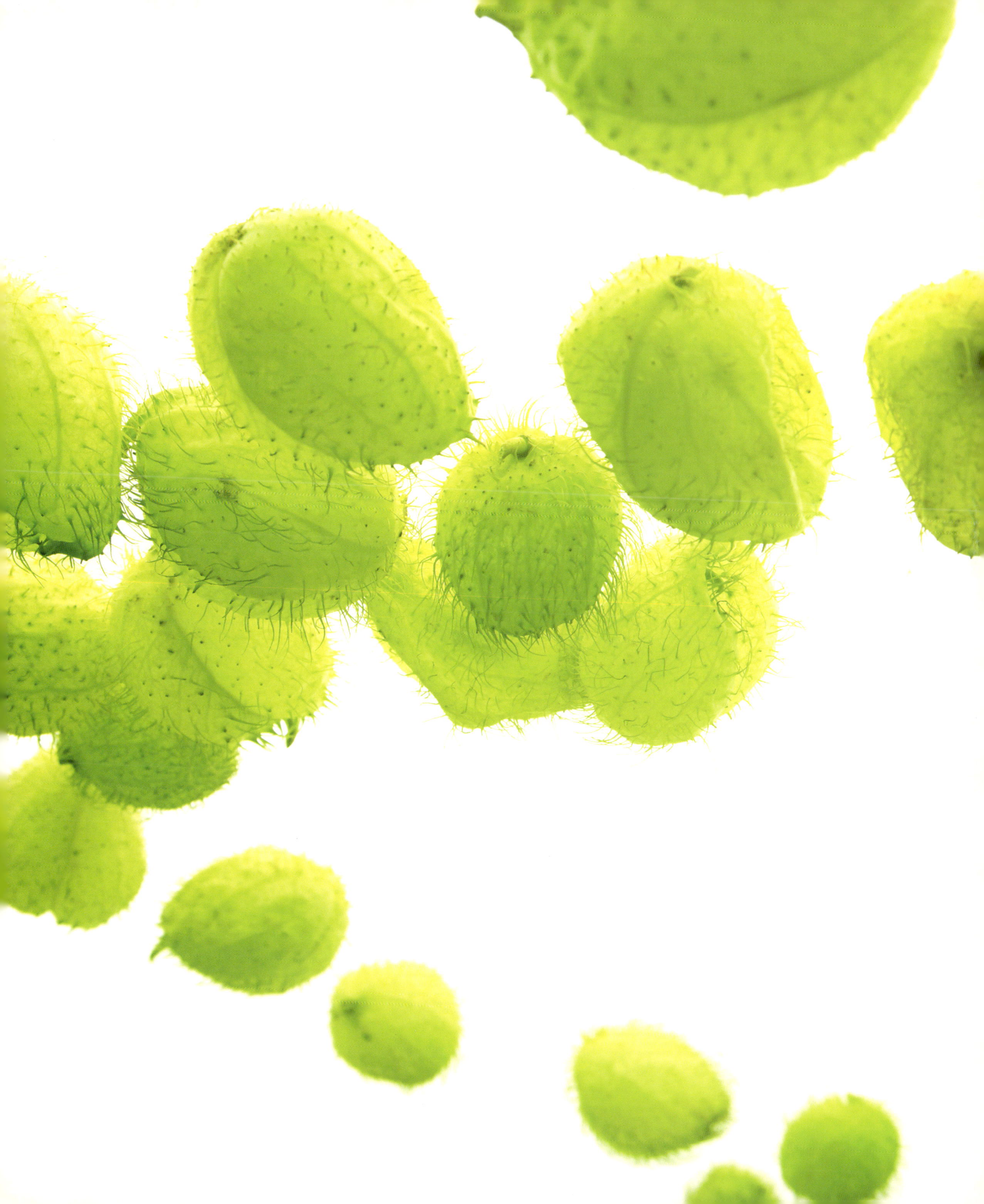

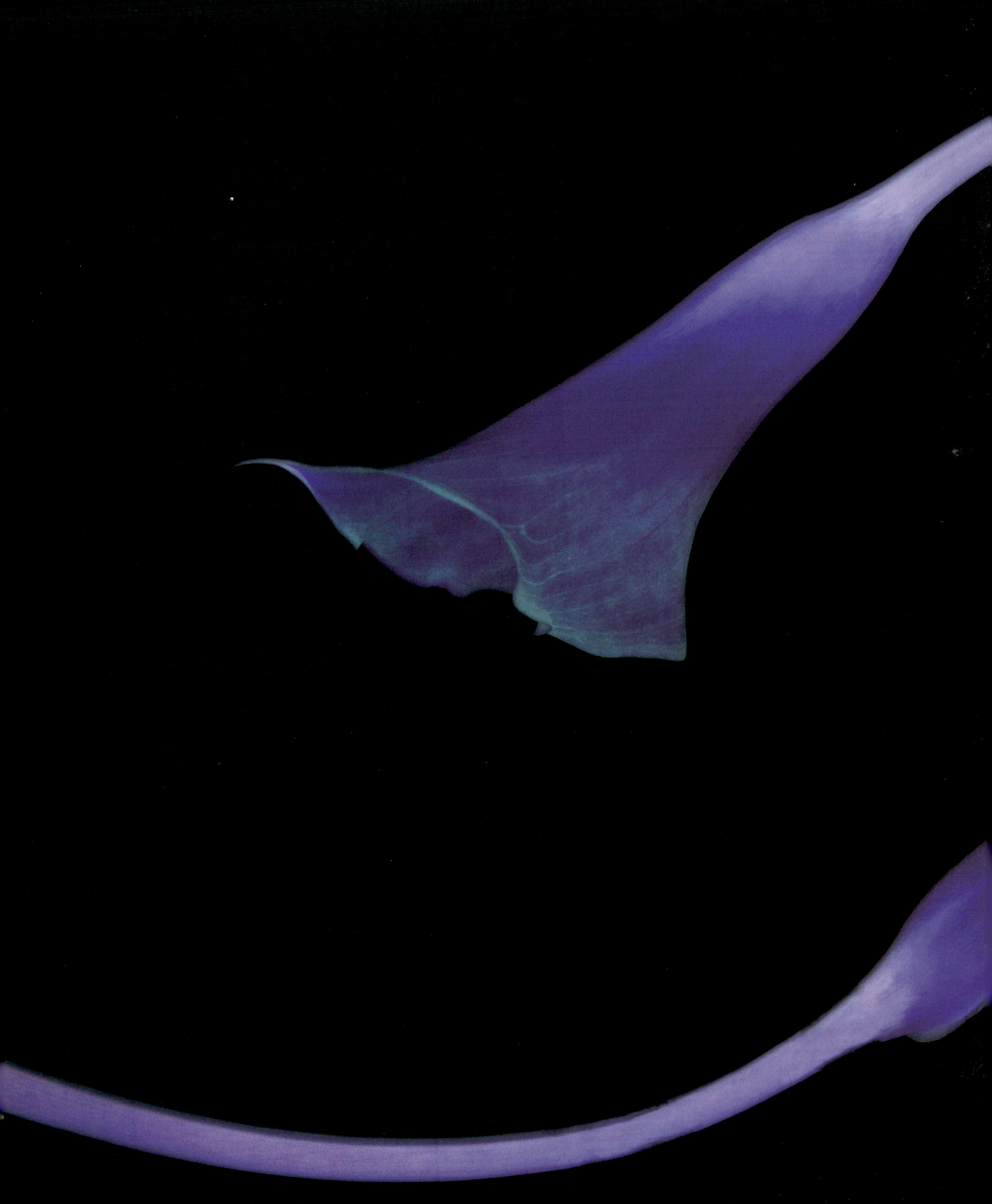

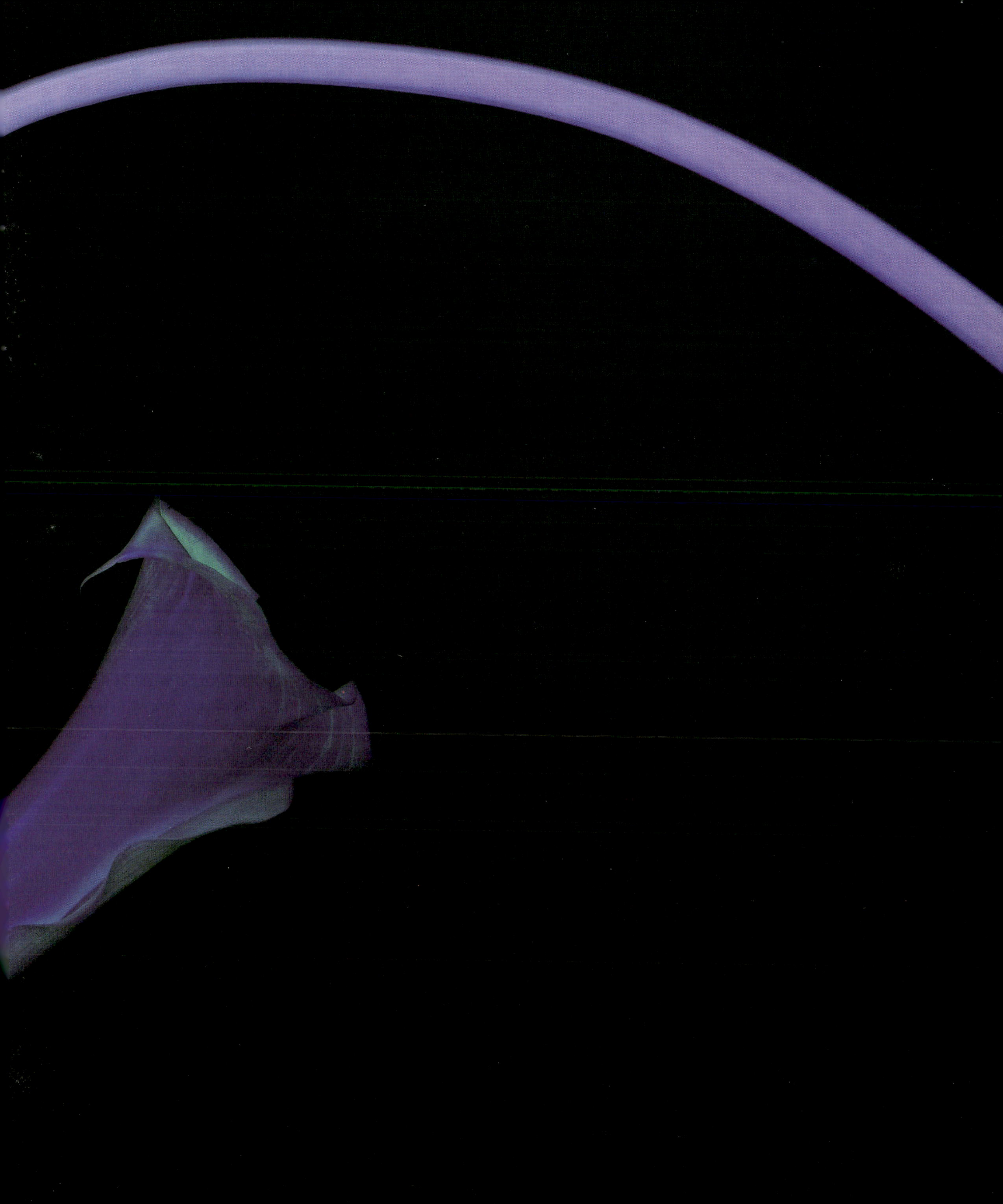

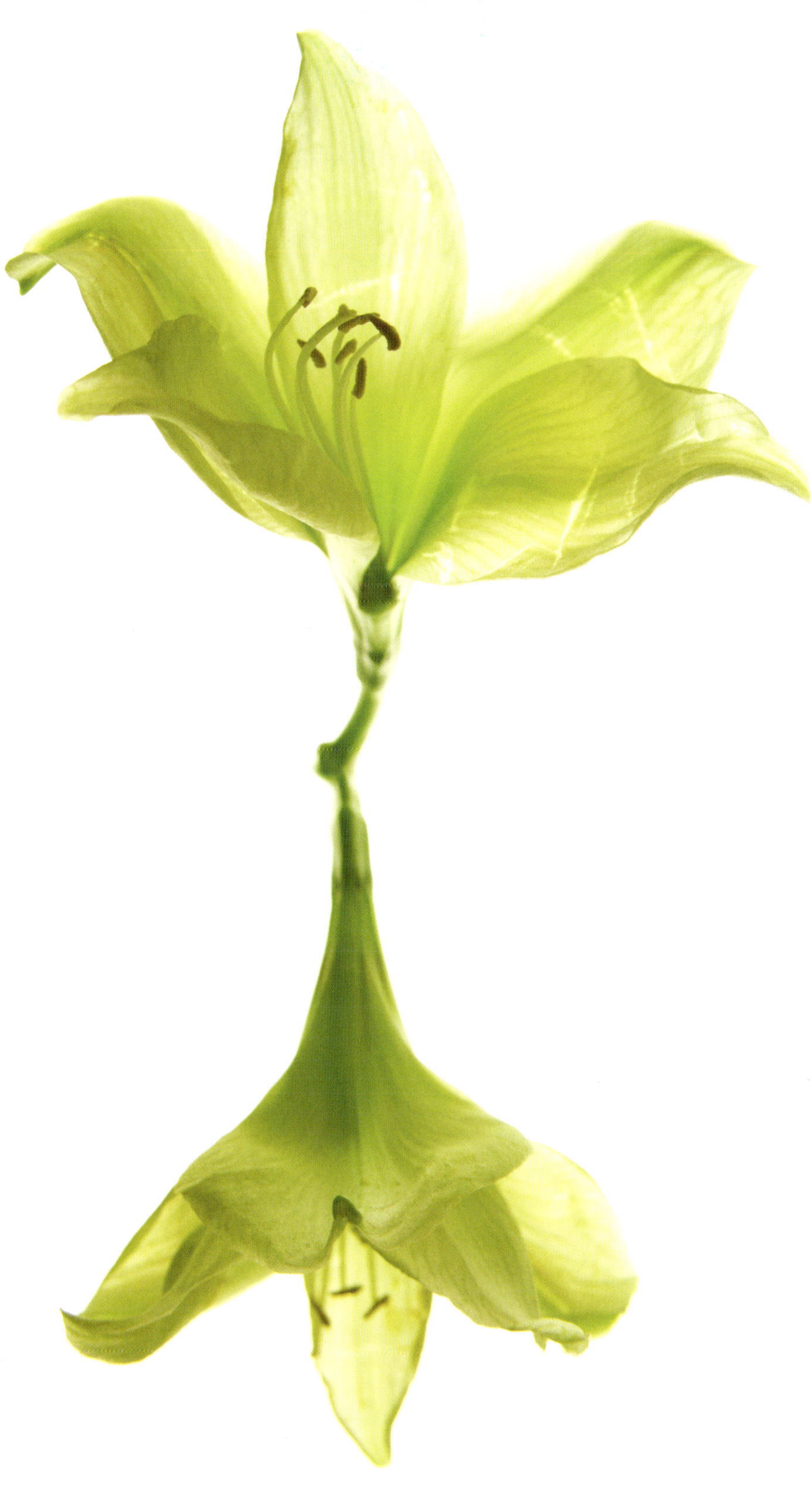

INDEX

Cover
Rosa species

Page 5
Gerbera species

Page 6
Narcissus species

Page 8
Jasminum plyanthum

Page 9
Astilbe chinensis

Page 11
Rudbeckia hirta

Page 12
Chamaedorea erumpens

Page 13
Rudbeckia lista

Pages 14-15
Rosa 'Candy Bianca'

Page 16
Tulipa x hybrida

Page 17
Rosa 'Akito'

Pages 18 and 19
Zantedeschia aethiopica

Page 20
Dendranthema 'Shamrock'

Page 21
Gerbera species

Page 22
Rosa species

Page 23
Eucalyptus cinerea

Page 24
Tulipa x hybrida

Page 25
Rosa 'Orange Unique'

Page 26
Hyacinthus orientalis

Page 27
Ranunculus asiaticus

Page 28
Cymbidium x hybrida

Page 29
Rosa 'Akito'

Page 30
Tulipa x hybrida

Page 31
Zantedeschia aethiopica

Page 32
Rosa 'Femma'

Page 33
Dahlia species

Pages 34-35
Phalaenopsis species

Page 36
Tulipa x hybrida

Page 37
Hyacinthus orientalis

Page 38
Anemone coronaria

Page 39
Lilium x hybrida 'Stargazer'

Page 40
Dendranthema species

Page 41
Rosa 'Akito'

Page 42
Cymbidium x hybrida

Page 43
Cattleya species

Page 44
Zantedeschia aethiopica

Page 45
Tulipa x hybrida

Page 46
Lilium x hybrida

Page 47
Rosa 'Polo'

Page 48
Cymbidium x hybrida

Page 49
Zantedeschia aethiopica

Page 50
Paphiopedilum leeanum 'King Arthur'

Page 51
Astilbe chinensis

Page 52
Paphiopedilum leeanum 'King Arthur'

Page 53
Astilbe chinensis

Pages 54 and 55
Jasminum polyanthum

Pages 56 and 57
Tulipa x hybrida

Page 58
Lilium x hybrida

Page 59
Rosa 'Charlotte'

Pages 60-61
Dahlia species

Pages 62 and 63
Viola x Wittrockiana

Page 64
Rudbeckia hirta

Page 65
Dahlia species

Page 66
Rosa Garden Variety

Page 67
Rosa 'First Red'

Pages 68-69
Oucidium 'Golden Shower'

Page 70
Gerbera 'Siby'

Page 71
Catteleya species

Page 72
Nymphaeceae species

Page 73
Rosa species

Page 74
Rudbeckia hirta

Page 75
Paphiopedilum species

Page 76
Rudbeckia hirta

Page 77
Narcissus species

Page 78 and 79
Passiflora species

Page 80
Rosa species

Page 81
Tulipa x hybrida

Page 82
Tulipa x hybrida

Page 83
Rosa 'Lemon Lime'

Page 84
Tulipa x hybrida petals

Page 85
Tulipa x hybrida

Page 86 and 87
Zantedeschia aethiopica

Page 89
Euphorbia species

Page 90-91
Zantedeschia aethiopica

Page 93
Hippeastreum species

Glitterati
INCORPORATED

First published in the United States of America in 2005 by
Glitterati Incorporated
225 Central Park West
New York, New York 10024
www.GlitteratiIncorporated.com

First edition, 2005

Art directed by **CHRISTOPHER MAKOS**
Design **PABLO GARCIA PEREZ**

Library of Congress Control Number:
2005930369

Hardcover ISBN 0-9765851-3-8

Printed and bound in China by Hong Kong Graphics & Printing Ltd.

10 9 8 7 6 5 4 3 2 1